BEER

IS THE

ANSWER

...I don't remember the question

by

RAY FOLEY

SOURCEBOOKS HYSTERIA™
AN IMPRINT OF SOURCEBOOKS, INC.®
NAPERVILLE, ILLINOIS

Published by Sourcebooks, Inc.
P.O. Box 4410, Naperville, Illinois 60567-4410
(630) 961-3900
Fax: (630) 961-2168
www.sourcebooks.com

Library of Congress Cataloging-in-Publication Data

Foley, Ray.
  Beer is the answer-- I don't remember the question / Ray Foley.
      p. cm.
  ISBN 978-1-4022-0914-7 (trade pbk.)
  1. Drinking of alcoholic beverages--Humor. 2. Drinking of alcoholic beverages--Quotations, maxims, etc. 3. Drinking customs--Humor. 4. Drinking customs--Quotations, maxims, etc. I. Title.

PN6231.D7F65 2007
818'.602--dc22
                                    2007021509

Printed and bound in the United States of America.
VG 10 9 8 7 6 5 4 3 2 1

To the 148,000 plus readers of BARTENDER Magazine and the thousands of bartenders who sent us jokes and quotes via our website www.bartender.com.

To Bob Schochet, for the fabulous cartoons.

And especially to Jaclyn Marie and Ryan Peter Foley, as well as the Other Tribe Members, Raymond, William, and Amy

BEER IS THE ANSWER
...I Don't Remember the Question

"Gimme a double whisky!," the little boy yelled to the barmaid as he entered the bar. "Do you want to get me in trouble?" she asked. "Maybe later," said the boy, "but right now, I'll just take the drink."

> ### "Never delay the ending of a meeting or the beginning of a cocktail hour."
> — [Anonymous]

> ### "Memorial services are the cocktail parties of the geriatric set."
> — Harold MacMillan

> ### "Wine gives courage and makes men more apt for passion."
> — Ovid

Have you ever noticed that at cocktail parties the men are usually standing around getting stiff while their wives are getting tight; but when they get home they find that neither is either?

> **"Forsake not an old friend, for the new is not comparable unto him. A new friend is as new wine: when it is old thou shalt drink it with pleasure."**
> — The Bible

> **"Never offer a drink without a smile."**
> — Pinchin

The inebriated university professor staggered into the bar and asked the bartender for a dry martinus. "Beg your pardon sir," the bartender said, "but don't you mean a martini?"

"Now see here, my good man," said the 90-proof prof, "If I want two, I'll ask for them."

~~~~~

"Me mother-in law's gone to her final reward," said Donnegan to the barkeep in Tamney's tavern, "and it's a twenty spot I'm needin' for a wreath. Could you be advancin' me the twenty?" The bartender emptied his pockets and the cash register, but the total came to only $18.30. "That'll do," said Donnegan, "I'll take the $1.70 in drinks!"

The beautiful blonde was talking with her handsome date in a posh restaurant when their waiter, stumbling as he brought their drinks, dumped a martini on the rocks down the back of the blonde's dress. She jumped to her feet, dashed wildly around the table, then galloped wriggling from the room followed by her distraught boyfriend. A man seated on the other side of the room with a date of his own beckoned to the waiter and said, "We'll have two of whatever she was drinking!"

> **"It is better for pearls to pass through the lips of swine than good wine to pass through the lips of the indifferent."**
> — Mark Luedtke
>
>
>
> **"If it is not true, it is a happy invention."**
> —Anonymous

COUNSEL: (to police witness) "So if a man is on his hands and knees in the middle of the road, that does not prove he is drunk?"

POLICE WITNESS: "No, sir, it does not. But this one was trying to roll up the white line."

CHEERS!

> ## "Growl all day and you'll feel dog tired at night."
> —Anonymous

> ## "He who doesn't risk, never gets to drink champagne."
> — Russian Proverb

Three deaf-mutes walked into a tavern and sat down at a table. The bartender greets them and takes their order using sign language. After returning to the bar he was complimented by a patron on his knowledge of sign language just to better serve his patrons. After a few rounds of drinks the bartender noticed the three deaf-mutes' hands moving a mile a minute. He quickly grabbed a bat from under the bar and chased the deaf-mutes out. When he returned, he was questioned by the same patron who complimented him earlier about why he ran them out of the bar.

He replied, "if I told them once, I told them a thousand times, no singing in this joint!"

—WILLIAM WEBB, MASTIC, N.Y.

Three asparagus were walking down the street when a car went out of control and hit one of them. The other two rushed their friend to the hospital. As they sat waiting for some news, a doctor came out and addressed them. "I have some good news and some bad news," he said. "First the good news, your friend will live. Now the bad news, he'll live the rest of his life as a vegetable."

—JOHN KIRST, NEWARK, NJ

"Only Irish coffee provides in a single glass all four essential food groups: alcohol, caffeine, sugar, and fat."

— Alex Levine

"Whatever you do, do cautiously, and look to the end."

—Anonymous

A drunk was trying to sneak into bed without arousing his hot-tempered wife. On route he paused in the kitchen and laboriously tied all the pots, pans, and trays he could find to a rope. He then proceeded upstairs, dragging the rope behind him, muttering happily, "She'll never hear me in all this racket."

I **had eighteen bottles of whisky** in my cellar and was told by my wife to empty the contents of each and every bottle down the sink, or else. I said I would and proceeded with the unpleasant task. I withdrew the cork from the first bottle and poured the contents down the sink with the exception of one glass which I drank. I extracted the cork from the second bottle and did likewise with the exception of one glass which I drank. I then withdrew the cork from the third bottle and poured the whisky down the sink which I drank. I pulled the cork from the fourth bottle down the sink and poured and poured the bottle down the glass which I drank. I pulled the bottle from the cork of the next and drank the sink out of it and threw the rest down the glass. I pulled the sink out of the next glass and poured the cork down the bottle. Then I corked the sink with the glass, bottled the drink and drank the pour.

When I had everything emptied, I steadied the house with one hand, counted the glasses, corks, bottles and sink with the other, which were 29, and as the house came by, I counted them again and finally had all the houses in one bottle, which I drank.

I'm not under the afluence of incohol, as some tinkle peep I am. I'm not half as thunk as you might drink. I fool so feelish I don't know who is me, and the drunker I stand here the longer I get.

An old couple sit down at a bar in the south, and the bartender strikes up a conversation with the man.

"Where y'all from?" The bartender asks.

"Chicago," the man replies.

The old man's hateful wife, who is partially deaf, pokes him in the ribs and screeches, "What'd he say? What'd he say?"

Exasperated, the old man shouts, "He just wanted to know where we were from."

"I've only been to Chicago once," the bartender says. "I had a one-night stand there—the worst sex I've ever had."

"What'd he say?" the wife screams.

The old man cups his hand to his mouth and yells back, "He thinks he knows ya!"

> **"Never refuse to do a kindness unless the act would work great injury to yourself, and never refuse to take a drink...under any circumstance."**
>
> — Mark Twain

CUSTOMER: "I say, bartender, isn't it a lovely day?"
BARTENDER: "Have you come here to drink or just talk?"

HAVE ANOTHER!

> "If I had to choose between putting a saloon or a liberal church on a corner, I'd choose the saloon every time. People who drink up the pay check in the saloon are less likely to become Pharisees, thinking that they don't need the Great Physician, than those who weekly swill the soporific doctrine of man's goodness."
>
> — Jay Edward Adams (b. 1929), American writer

The big man approached the bartender and said, "I see by the sign in your window that you're looking for a bouncer. Has the job been filled yet?"

"Not yet," the bartender replied, "do you have experience?"

"No," the man admitted, "but watch this!"

He walked over to a loudmouthed drunk at the back of the room, lifted him off his feet, and threw him out into the street. Then he turned to the bartender and said, "How's that?"

"Great!" said the bartender, "but you'll have to ask the boss about the job."

"Fine," said the man, "Where is he?"

"Just coming back in the front door."

A pair of intoxicated buddies were seated in their favorite bar drinking their favorite drinks. "I think I'll have a bite to eat," said the first inebriated fellow. He suddenly took the olive from his martini and ate it.

"Ah!," said his sozzled companion. "That calls for an after-dinner drink!"

~~~~~

Then there's the one about the customer who fell down four flights of stairs with two quarts of vodka and didn't spill a drop, just by keeping his mouth shut.

~~~~~

"Is it true," asked the customer, "that alcohol makes people able to do things better?"

"No," replied the bartender, "it just makes them less ashamed of doing them badly."

"Know thyself."

—Anonymous

"Never take a beer to a job interview."

— Anonymous

It was a quiet day in heaven, so God and Saint Peter decided to play a round of golf. God put the ball on a tee, addressed the ball, and hit a perfect shot, headed right down the fairway. Suddenly the ball was swept away by a fierce gust of wind. A passing bird grabbed the ball in its mouth and flew back towards the fairway. A sudden crash of thunder caused the frightened bird to drop the ball out of its mouth. The ball landed in trees and bounced from tree to tree to tree, until it finally bounced off the back of a passing turtle, hit a rock, and landed on the back of a rabbit. The startled rabbit ran from the woods toward the green. The ball fell off the rabbit's back and rolled towards the hole. The ball circled the rim of the cup three times and finally fell in the hole. Saint Peter turned to God and said, "Did we come here to play golf or to fart around?"

—SCOTT CAMPBELL, THE MANOR, WEST ORANGE, NJ

"I just can't find a cause for your illness," the internist said. "Frankly, I think it's due to drinking."

"In that case," replied his patient, "I'll come back when you're sober."

~~~

A man walked into the local pub with a frog atop his head. The startled bartender asked, "Hey, where did you get that?" The frog croaked, "Would you believe it started out as a wart on my ass?"

A drunk standing at a bar ordered a cocktail, drank it, then started chewing and swallowing the glass up to the stem. He noticed the fellow looking at him. "Who you looking at? What is it to you?"

"Nothing," came the drunken reply. "But why do you leave the stem? That's the best part!"

> ## "Solomon made a book of proverbs, but a book of proverbs never made a Solomon."
>
> —Anonymous
>
>
>
> ## "If you see in your wine the reflection of a person not in your range of vision, don't drink it."
>
> — Chinese Proverb

DOCTOR: "The best thing for you to do is to give up drinking and smoking, get up early every morning and go to bed early every night."

PATIENT: "What's the second best thing to do?"

ANOTHER ROUND!

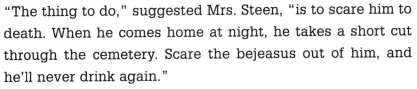

> ## "A wise man knows everything; a shrewd one, everybody."
>
> —Anonymous
>
>
>
> ## "One drink is just right; two is too many; three are too few."
>
> — Spanish Proverb

"The thing to do," suggested Mrs. Steen, "is to scare him to death. When he comes home at night, he takes a short cut through the cemetery. Scare the bejeasus out of him, and he'll never drink again."

So Mrs. Mcardle rented a devil's costume and hid behind a tombstone in the cemetery. That night, as Mcardle stumbled by, she jumped out and growled: "Ahh, ah, ah!"

"Who are you?" slobbered Mcardle.

"I am the devil!"

"Shake hands; I'm married to your sister!"

You know you like to drink when:

➤ you tell people it only takes you one drink to make you drunk, but you're not sure it's the ninth or tenth.

➤ you get so lit up from drinking that people read by you during blackouts.

➤ you drink so much that you can hear the pretzels splash as you eat them.

➤ people start calling you "truck" because you always have a load on.

➤ your boss asks you to work overtime and you demand time and a fifth.

➤ the only thing your health means to you is something to drink to.

➤ you want to have your elbows furrowed so they won't slip off the wet bars.

➤ you're afraid of being killed by a flask of lightning.

➤ you're expelled from alcoholics anonymous because you're not anonymous enough to suit them.

➤ someone calls you a fried egghead and you think they mean an alcoholic intellectual.

➤ you say you're on a balanced diet and you mean a high-ball in each hand.

➤ the bartender warns you not to stand up while the room's in motion.

➤ you tell the story of how you were held up on your way home, when in fact, that's the only way you could have gotten home.

A man stepped into a crowded bar and ordered a beer. After a short while he had to go to the men's room. In order not to have his beer stolen, he put a note on the glass reading, "I spat in this beer."

When he returned there was a footnote added, "So did I!"

—GUIDO MATERA, SOMERSET HILLS COUNTRY CLUB, BERNARDSVILLE, NJ

"If you can't win, make the fellow ahead of you break the record."

—Anonymous

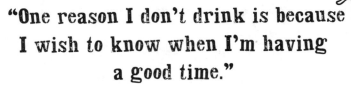

"One reason I don't drink is because I wish to know when I'm having a good time."

— Nancy Astor (1879-1964), English stateswoman

"I never drink water. I'm afraid it will become habit-forming."

— W.C. Fields (1880-1946), American actor and comedian

A **veteran of World War II** walked into a tavern and ordered two scotch and waters. The bartender complied. After the customer repeated the order for many months, the bartender suggested that he order a double scotch and water. This did not satisfy the customer and he continued with the same order, two scotch and waters. Then one day the customer appeared and instead of ordering two scotch and waters, he ordered just one. This continued for a number of days until the bartender wanted his curiosity satisfied and asked, "How come you used to order two of them and now you order just one?" He answered, "One drink was for me and the other for my buddy, in his memory because he was killed in action. But since the doctor advised me not to have a drink, I'm taking this one for my buddy."

—JOEL SIMON, PRIME MOTOR INNS, CLIFTON, NJ

belly buster!

> **"The first drink with water, the second without water, the third like water."**
> — Spanish Proverb

> **"A diplomat is a man who remembers a lady's birthday but forgets her age."**
> —Anonymous

Don't drink and drive. You just might hit a bump and spill it.

~~~~~

Asked by his teacher to spell "straight," the third grade boy did so without error. "Now," said the teacher, "what does it mean?"

"Without water."

> ## "Noble ancestry makes a poor dish at table."
> —Anonymous

> ## "A man must defend his wife, his home, his children and his martini."
> — Jackie Gleason

> ## "It takes time to be a woman."
> —Anonymous

They offered the great drinker grapes for dessert.

"No thank you!" said he, pushing back the plate. "I don't take wine in pills!"

"I was married twice," explained the man to a newly discovered drinking companion. "and I'll never marry again. My first wife died after eating poison mushrooms and my second died of a fractured skull."

"That's a shame," offered the friend, "how did that happen?"

"She wouldn't eat her mushrooms."

> **"The most important things to do in the world are to get something to eat, something to drink and somebody to love you."**
>
> — Brendan Francis Behan (1923-64),
> Irish writer, playwright
>
> ---
>
> **"Prosperity makes friends and adversity tries them."**
>
> —Anonymous

You know you like to drink when:

....someone asks your nationality and you answer that you're half scotch and half shot most of the time.

CHEERS!

> "Let's drink to the spirit of gallantry and courage that made a strange Heaven out of unbelievable Hell, and let's drink to the hope that one day this country of ours, which we love so much, will find dignity and greatness and peace again."
>
> — Noel Coward

Borderline ZANY!

The morning after, a man was attempting to tell his wife where he was when he got loaded. All he could remember was that it was a club with a green door, purple walls, and a gold commode.

The wife, a skeptical sort, wouldn't believe that. She got on the phone and called up every cocktail lounge and nightspot in the yellow pages. Finally she reached the last club listed, and lo and behold. Found out it did have a green front door, and yes, their walls were painted purple. She then asked about the gold commode. The bartender who answered the phone motioned for the manager. "Hey Charlie, come here quick. I think we found the guy who barfed in the tuba last night!"

A drunk searching along the edge of the pavement and the gutter was approached by an officer who said: "What you looking for, me boy?"

"I just lost a buck."

"Where did you lose it, now?"

"About two blocks down the street."

"Then, now, why are you looking here?"

"Oh," replied the drunk, "the light is much better here."

"Nothing in excess."

—Anonymous

"A gentleman is a man who can disagree without being disagreeable."

—Anonymous

A bum walked into a very chic pub and ordered a beer. Discreetly, the bartender informed him, "We do not serve riff raff here."

To which the bum responded, "Then what brands do you serve here?"

—PETER BONANNO

"If at first you don't succeed, destroy all evidence that you tried."
—Anonymous

"Drink and the whole world drinks with you; stop and you sit alone!"
—Cliff, Cheers

A man rushed excitedly into the tavern and shouted: "A lady just fainted outside! Does anybody have a shot of whiskey?" The bartender instantly filled a glass and handed it to the man, and said "On the house."

The stranger grabbed the glass, downed its contents and handed it back to the bartender. "Thanks," he said, "I always get sick when I see someone faint."

One afternoon a middle-class man left the local watering hole and started home. Looking into the street he saw the strangest thing. Two big black limousines were driving slowly down the street, followed by a man walking the biggest, meanest looking dog he'd ever seen. Following behind the man and dog were a group of about 20 men. Puzzled by this he walked over and questioned the dog owner. He asked, "What's going on here?"

The dog owner looked at him, smiled, and pointed to the limousines. He said, "you see that first limousine? That's my dead wife."

"That's too bad, "replied the first man.

"Do you see that second limousine? That's my mother-in-law, she's dead also. Do you see this dog? This dog killed the both of them."

"That's terrible!" shouted the first man. Suddenly, he grinned and took the man with the dog to the side and whispered in his ear, "Can I borrow your dog?"

The dog owner smiled and pointed to the men walking behind him, "Sure, just go wait in line."

—WILLIAM FULLER, BOONTON, NJ

"Your ticket," declared the conductor to the intoxicated passenger after examining the latter's ticket, "is for Newark and this train is on the Ohio line and doesn't go through Newark."

"Good grief!" exclaimed the intoxicated one. "Have you told the engineer?"

A hardworking Irish wife came to her priest with the tale of her husband, his constant drinking, and his terribly late hours. The priest was kindly and suggested that he talk to her husband the first chance he had.

One morning, sometime later, the priest sat down on a street corner beside McGee, who was buried in the morning paper. He looked up, greeted the priest, and then continued reading. The father waited and finally McGee looked up again.

"Say, father, what causes an ulcer?"

Here was his chance, the priest thought.

"Well, my son, it is sinful living. Constant drinking and keeping late hours. Why do you ask?"

"Well, Father, it says here that the pope has one!"

> **"I see where New York is going to make their nightclubs close at three in the morning, and the people are kicking about it. Well, I say they ought to close 'em. Anybody that can't get drunk by three A.M. ain't trying."**
>
> — Will Rogers

Clancy went into a pub and ordered a beer. He drank half, then threw the rest at the bartender. Clancy apologized, explaining it was a compulsion he's had for years that embarrassed him terribly. The barkeeper told him to see a psychiatrist and warned him not to come back until he had done so.

A few months later, Clancy again entered the bar and ordered a brew. He drank half and threw the rest all over the bartender.

"I told you not to come back here until you'd seen a shrink about your compulsion!" the bartender yelled.

"I have been seeing one," replied Clancy indignantly.

"Well, it hasn't done any good," roared the dripping bartender.

"Yes, it has," said Clancy. "I'm not embarrassed about it anymore."

> ## "I hate to advocate drugs, alcohol, violence, or insanity to anyone, but they've always worked for me."
>
> — Hunter S. Thompson

Two brothers came into my bar for a drink. They ordered two drinks and one brother asked, "How much?" I said two dollars, so he put two bottle caps on the bar and went to the men's room. His brother told me not to worry because his brother had just come from the nuthouse and that he would pay the check. A little later he asked for the bill and I told him again, two dollars.

He stood up, zipped open his jacket, and tossed a hub cap on the bar and said, "Do you have change of a fifty?"

—RICHARD GUERTIN

"I love to sing, and I love to drink scotch. Most people would rather hear me drink scotch."

— George Burns

"Every dog is entitled to one bite."

—Anonymous

WIFE: "What did you get drunk for in the first place?"

HUSBAND: "I didn't get drunk in the first place. I got drunk in the last place."

HAVE ANOTHER!

From Conan McCarty in New York City, this is a three-part joke:

Quasimodo has retired. The priest holds interviews and auditions to fill the vacancy, to which a man with no arms shows up. The priest asked how he intended to ring the bell. The man replied: "With my face," the skeptical priest laughed, the man backed up, ran full tilt at the bell and smacked it with the bridge of his nose. "That's all well and good," replied the priest, "but my congregation is spread out over 10 miles. I've got to have volume." The man asked for a second chance, backed up farther, ran hell bent for leather and careened into the bell, which gave a high resonant bong, but unfortunately the man ricocheted off the left side and fell off the parapet to his death. The priest ran downstairs to the crowd surrounding the writhing body. People asked him: "Father do you know who this is?" "Well, I don't know his name, but his face rings a bell."

Three days later, a second man with no arms showed up for the same job. The priest refused the man admittance, saying he didn't want to go through that again. "What do you mean, again?"

"Three days ago another no-arm guy shows..." "That's my brother! I've been following him for years! How's he doing?"

The priest told him how his brother had unfortunately passed away, whereupon the man urged the priest to hire him so he could dedicate the remainder of his life working where his brother had passed away. "I've corrected the fault he had on his approach to the bell," he said, "so just let me work here for my brother." The priest hesitated, so the man backed up and hurled himself into the bell, which gave a resplendent bong, but the man fell off the right side of the bell, off the parapet to the courtyard below. The priest rushed downstairs.

Startled onlookers asked, "Do you know this one, father?"

"No, but he's a dead ringer for his brother."

Now, several people have told me there is a third part. I've searched in vain. (You Hymie, are my last hope!) Following are two responses to McCarty's Quasimodo joke. We're printing both to give our readers a choice of which ending they think fits the joke best.

Several days later the third brother shows up for the job and asks the priest if he can ring the bell. The man hurls himself at the bell, but no sound; a second time he hurls himself at the bell, but no sound. The third time he hurls himself at the bell, still no sound, but he falls off the parapet to the courtyard below. The priest rushes downstairs and the startled onlookers ask: "Do you know this one father?!"

"No, but he's a deadbeat like his two brothers."

—CHUCK KEINER, IL

First of all, the story starts with Quasimodo wanting to retire. He places an ad in the paper and interviews an armless dwarf. From there on the stories (#1 and #2) are similar except that they are far funnier when the story teller acts out the part of Quasimodo trudging down the spiral staircase from Notre Dame's bell tower with the hump on his back. Here is the third part.

After the second armless dwarf falls off the tower, Quasi (to his friends) places another ad in the paper and a third, armless dwarf shows up, the third brother. Once again, Quasi explains the rigors of the job and impresses on the dwarf that the "gong" has to be heard all over the city. The dwarf answers quasi he can do it and is given a try out. He goes back as far as he can, speeds towards the great bell at an alarming rate, misses the bell completely, goes off the tower and smashes to the street below. Quasi jumps down the spiral staircase and when asked by the crowd if he knows the man, states: "No, I don't know his name and his face doesn't ring a bell with me."

—CATHY STRAUMAN, NY

"A taxpayer is someone who does not have to pass a civil service exam to work for the government."

—Anonymous

"THAT'S IT. IT'S BARTENDER
SCHOOL FOR YOU!"

"I once shook hands with Pat Boone and my whole right side sobered up."

— Dean Martin (1917-1995) American singer and actor

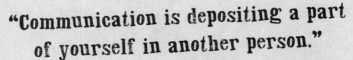

"Communication is depositing a part of yourself in another person."

—Anonymous

A drunk confides to his bartender that he is getting a divorce after just three days of marriage because his new wife is in the hospital. "Just because she's sick is no reason to divorce her," says the bartender. "I should'da never married her," moans the drunk, "she said she had a tape worm and I thought she said tap room."

"Adversity introduces a man to himself."

—Anonymous

Father Murphy was a priest of a very poor parish and asked several people for suggestions on raising money for his church. He was told that race horses always make money, so he went to the horse auction. However, he got a very poor deal, for the purchase turned out to be a donkey. However, he thought he might as well enter his donkey in the race. The donkey came in third and next day the paper carried this headline: "Father Murphy's ass shows." The archbishop saw this and was very displeased. The next day the donkey came in first and the headlines read: "Father Murphy's ass out in front." The archbishop was aghast at this and didn't know what to do. Again the donkey entered the race and came in second. This time the headlines read: "Father Murphy's ass back in place." This was too much, so the archbishop forbade Father Murphy from entering the donkey again. The next day the headlines read: "Archbishop scratches Father Murphy's ass."

> **"Drinking is in reality an occupation which employs a considerable portion of the time of many people; and to conduct it in the most rational and agreeable."**
>
> — James Boswell

A doctor and his wife were dining at the local tavern one evening when a stunning redhead at a nearby table recognized the doctor and waved at him. Noticing the look on his wife's face, the doctor said soothingly, "Just someone I met professionally, dear."

"I'm sure," replied the wife, "but, yours or hers?"

> ## "Some drink at the fountain of knowledge...others just gargle."
>
> —Anonymous

> ## "What we want is standard time for getting up and daylight saving time for quitting work."
>
> —Anonymous

She left her gloves in the bar, discovered her loss at the door and went back to her booth. Not finding them on the table, she got down an all fours searching underneath. The bartender walked over, bent down and whispered to her, "If you're looking for your husband, ma'am, you'll be glad to know he made it to a cab."

ANOTHER ROUND!

> "Of course I don't always enjoy being a mother. At these times my husband and I hole up somewhere in the wine country, eat, drink, make mad love and pretend we were born sterile and raise poodles."
>
> — Dorothy DeBolt

WIFE: "Here is another terrible effect of alcohol right here in the paper. Mr. Smith got into a boat and shoved out into the river. Being drunk from drinking whisky, he upset the boat, fell into the river and drowned. Now if he hadn't drunk the whisky he would still be alive today."

HUSBAND: "Let me see. He fell into the river, didn't he?"

WIFE: "Yes, he did."

HUSBAND: "Then he didn't die till he fell in?"

WIFE: "Of course not!

HUSBAND: "Then it was the water that killed him, not the whisky."

~~~~

The marine was being questioned where his money went:

"Part for booze, part for women, and the rest spent foolishly."

"It is alcohol, and alcohol alone, that is responsible for your present position," said the judge to the drunk.

Said the drunk, "Thank you, your honor, for sayin' that. You're the first person that hasn't said it was all my fault."

"A friend is one who dislikes the same people that you dislike."

—Anonymous

"Drink to me only with thine eyes. And I will pledge with mine; Or leave a kiss but in the cup. And I'll not look for wine."

— Ben Jonson (1573-1637)

"A narrow mind and a wide mouth usually go together."

—Anonymous

A drunk stumbles into a confessional. The priest hears him come in, but he hears nothing else. So the priest knocks on the wall. The drunk mumbles. "Forget it, buddy...there's no paper in this one either!"

I t was the middle shift in the lounge at the Shamrock Hilton as the duty bartender did his afternoon side work and he was the only one in the room. Though his back was to the door. The back bar mirror told that a lovely, well-dressed young lady was on the way to the bar. As she seated herself, he turned and smiled

"Good afternoon. Scotch and water?"

She said, "Why, that's marvelous! How did you know? I've never been here before!"

"Oh, I'm just a smart bartender" he replied. He went about his duties, and as she finished her drink he looked up and said, "Gin and tonic?" She was amazed! "How on earth did you know?" she asked. Again he replied, "I'm just a smart bartender."

This dialogue continued through two more drinks; each time she changed drinks, and each time he had the same answer. Finally he said, "I even know what you do for a living. You're a hooker."

Though startled, she answered, "How on earth did you know?" Same answer, "Well, I'm just a smart bartender."

She recouped her composure and asked, "My God, is there anything you don't know?" "Well, yes" our friend replied, "I've always wondered, do hookers have babies?"

She never batted an eyelash. "Sure," she said. "Where do you think all the smart bartenders come from?"

—WALT COLEMAN, TX

> **"Drunkenness does not create vice;
> it merely brings it into view."**
>
> — Seneca
>
> ——— 🍻 ———
>
> **"The really happy man is one who
> can enjoy the scenery on a detour."**
>
> —Anonymous

Strange things can happen to good friends of the grape – and often do.

Like the experience of the couple who were teetering on adjoining bar stools, starting their twelfth Tom Collins of the evening, when the husband said: "Your mother has been living with us for two years now. Don't you think it's time she got a place of her own?"

"My mother?!" The wife shrieked. "I thought she was your mother!"

> **"If you wish to know what a man is,
> place him in authority."**
>
> —Anonymous

The difference between a rich drunk and a poor one is that a rich one tells his problems to a psychiatrist and a poor one tells his to a bartender.

~~~~~

The star said, "Doc, there's something wrong with me. When I go down into my cellar, I feel fine. But when I come back up I feel dizzy, tired, and have trouble keeping my balance. What is it?" The doc said, "I'm not sure – but I'll bet it's a wine cellar."

> **"An expert is a person who can take something you already know and make it sound confusing."**
>
> —Anonymous

Here's a ZINGER!

> **"Fishing, with me, has always been an excuse to drink in the daytime."**
>
> — Jimmy Cannon

> **"I've drunk wine for seventy-five years, and I never drink water. I have a constitution of iron, and water rusts iron."**
>
> — Andre L. Simon

Enjoy A FROSTY MUG BEER!

> **"We are in such a slump that even the ones that aren't drinking aren't hittin'."**
> – Casey Stengel
>
>
>
> **"An optimist is a person who starts a crossword puzzle with a fountain pen."**
> —Anonymous

A regular patron at Rusty's Bar reports that he and his girl can't seem to agree on wedding plans. "She wants a big church wedding with ushers and bridegrooms, and I just don't want to get married."

~~~~

The tough guy sauntered into the dimly lit saloon. "Is there anybody here called Donovan?" He snarled. Nobody answered. Again he snarled, "Is there anybody here called Donovan?" There was a moment of silence and then a little fellow strode forward. "I'm Donovan," he said. The tough guy picked him up and threw him across the bar. Then he punched him in the jaw, kicked him, clubbed him, slapped him around a bit and walked out. About fifteen minutes later the little fellow came to. "Boy, did I fool him," he said. "I ain't Donovan."

> ## "Son, when you participate in sporting events, it's not whether you win or lose...it's how drunk you get."
>
> — Homer Simpson
>
>
>
> ## "The rich would have to eat money, but luckily the poor provide food."
>
> —Anonymous

A man wandered out of a bar. "Call me a cab," he said to a gentleman standing outside. "I am not a doorman," replied the man stiffly. "I am an officer in the United States Navy." "Fine," came the reply, "then call me a boat."

In one of those western scenes so familiar on TV, two groups of men were shooting it out in the barroom of a shabby roadhouse. Suddenly a meek little man entered the door and started right across the room toward the bar. All the shooting stopped. The bartender got up from behind the safety of the bar and said, "Partner, it sure took real courage to walk right through all those six guns without lookin' right nor left." "Not at all," replied the meek little man as he asked for a sarsaparilla. "You see, I owe money to everyone in the place."

A guy walks into a bar in Canada; sitting on one of the bar stools is a huge stuffed grizzly bear.

"Where did you get that bear?" asks the guy.

"I shot him when me and my uncle went out hunting last winter," says the bartender.

"What's he stuffed with?" asks the guy.

"My uncle."

> ## "If you resolve to give up smoking, drinking and loving, you don't actually live longer; it just seems longer."
>
> — Clement Freud
>
>
>
> ## "Each hour injures, the last one slays."
>
> —Anonymous

A seventy-year-old millionaire announces his engagement to an eighteen-year-old girl in Smitty's Bar. "Drinks are on me," the man says.

"Tell me," says Smitty, "I know you've got money. But how did you get a beautiful eighteen-year-old to marry you when you're seventy?"

"I told her I was ninety-five."

CHEERS!

...I Don't Remember the Question 43

Priceless!

The other day little **Johnny** ran into the kitchen and said, "Mommy, how old are you?" She said, "That's a personal question that you shouldn't ask people." Johnny then asked her, "Mommy, how much do you weigh?" With that she exclaimed, "You don't ask a woman those questions. Now you go outside and play."

Johnny went outside and played with his friends. After telling one of his friends about the questions he had asked his mom, his friend said he should get into his mom's wallet and check her driver's license, as it has all that information on it.

About an hour later, he strolled back into the kitchen and said to his mom, "Mommy, I know you're thirty-two years old."

Somewhat surprised, she asked how he know that. Without answering her question, he said, "And I know you weigh 128 pounds."

Now a bit annoyed, she said, "And how do you know that?"

Without answering again, he said, "And I know why you and daddy are divorced. You got an "f" in sex."

—JERRY C. GASBER. GASBER'S FINE FOOD, OH

"In the Bowling Alley of Tomorrow, there will even be machines that wear rental shoes and throw the ball for you. Your sole function will be to drink beer."

— Dave Barry

---

44 BEER IS THE ANSWER

Two cannibals walk into a bar and sit beside this clown. The first cannibal whacks the clown on the head and they both start eating the clown. Suddenly, the second cannibal looks up and says, "Hey, do you taste something funny?"

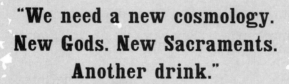

"We need a new cosmology. New Gods. New Sacraments. Another drink."

— Patti Smith

"Age and treachery will triumph over youth and skill."

—Anonymous

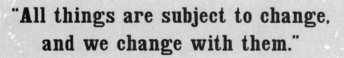

"All things are subject to change, and we change with them."

—Anonymous

A snake walks into a bar and the bartender says, "I'm sorry, but I can't serve you."

"Why not?" asks the snake.

"Because you can't hold your liquor."

Bartender asks customer: "What about the tip?"

Customer replies: "You want a tip? Don't get off a moving bus!!"

—Jason Williams, Cape Town, South Africa

"I never drink water, look at the way it rusts pipes."

—W. C. Fields

"When you get to the end of your rope, tie a knot and hang on."

—Anonymous

Cop: "Say, me boy, do you know who I am?"

Man: "I can't say as I do, but if you'll tell me where you live, I'll help you home."

Golden rules for easier living

➤ If you open it, close it.
➤ If you turn it on, turn it off.
➤ If you unlock it, lock it up.
➤ If you break it, admit it.
➤ If you can't fix it, call in someone who can.
➤ If you borrow it, return it.
➤ If you value it, take care of it.
➤ If you make a mess, clean it up.
➤ If you move it, move it back.
➤ If it belongs to someone else and you want to use it, get permission.
➤ If you don't know how to operate it, leave it alone.
➤ If it's none of your business, don't ask questions.
➤ If it isn't broken, don't fix it.
➤ If it will brighten someone's day—say it!

"I must get out of these wet clothes and into a dry martini."

—Robert Benchley

"Book lovers never go to bed alone."

—Anonymous

> **"It's a shame that the only thing a man can do for eight hours a day is work. He can't eat for eight hours; he can't drink for eight hours; he can't make love for eight hours. The only thing a man can do for eight hours is work."**
>
> — William Faulkner

A drunk finally finds the keyhole and enters into the house. Here, he stumbles looking for the lights. His wife finally wakes up and shouts, "Is that you, Fred?"

No answer. A big crash of glass. "Fred, what in the world are you doing?"

"Teaching your goldfish not to bark at me!"

—JOHN KNIGHT, LEGGETTS SAND BAR MANASQUAN, NJ

> **"A smile is a passport that will take you anywhere you want to go."**
>
> —Anonymous

 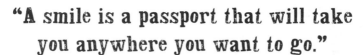

Discovering too late that a watermelon spiked with vodka had accidentally been served to a luncheon meeting of local ministers, the restaurant's owner waited nervously for the clerics' reaction.

"Quick, man," he whispered to his waiter, "what did they say?"

"Nothing," said the waiter. "They were all too busy slipping the seeds into their pockets."

> "Love, with very young people, is a heartless business. We drink at that age from thirst, or to get drunk; it is only later in life that we occupy ourselves with the individuality of our wine."
>
> — Emily Elizabeth Dickinson (1830-1886), American poet

A drunk at a bar asks the man next to him, "Djew just pour beer in my pocket?"

"No."

He asks everyone. They all deny it.

"Aha!" exclaims the drunk. "It'sh an inshide job!"

HAVE ANOTHER!

side splitter!

Last year, **New York** changed the drinking laws to age 19—now they want to make it legal for kids to drink at age twenty-one. Suppose the kids don't want to drink?

Why are we worried about raising the drinking age for youngsters? Let's lower the drinking age to save us from the old drunks.

Now, take Dean Martin. I wouldn't say he has a drinking problem, but his major concern in life is what wine goes with whiskey.

Would you believe Dean Martin's water bed has 38% alcohol content? Dean says, "Whiskey is good for insomnia—it may not put you to sleep but it makes you perfectly happy to stay awake."

Everybody is trying to find ways to get us loaded…would you believe candy with liquor in the middle? I heard one drunk ask, "Gimme a fifth of middles." Supermarkets will soon have drinks for everybody: 30-proof Alpo for dogs and Purina muscatel for your pet cat. In Hollywood, the cat food will be strictly champagne flavored, and the wine bags will be in decorator colors.

Ed McMahon says, "Liquor may not be the world's greatest medicine, but at least you can order it without a prescription." Ed's doctor told him he had to eat more—so now he has three olives with his martini.

I'll tell you something about Hollywood: they are way ahead of us in handling drunk drivers. They now have express lanes for those carrying six pints or less.

> ## "Even a stopped clock is right twice a day."
> —Anonymous

The bouncer threw the drunk out on his ear four times running, but the undaunted victim kept staggering back for more. A customer watched the performance with interest, and finally tapped the bouncer on the shoulder. "Know why that bum keeps coming back in?" He observed, "You're putting too much backspin on him."

> ## "The man who minds his own business usually has a good one."
> —Anonymous

> ## "A good drink makes the old young."
> — Proverb

To tell a woman who is forty she looks like sixteen is baloney. The blarney way of saying it is, "Tell me how old you are. I should like to know at what age women are most beautiful!"

> **"In water one sees one's own face; but in wine, one beholds the heart of another."**
> — old French proverb, courtesy of Bob Higgins

> **"Everybody must believe in something...
> I believe I'll have another drink."**
> — Murphy (of Murphy's Law fame)

The drunk staggered into the bar shouting, "Happy New Year, Happy New Year everybody!"

The guy closest to him said, "You idiot, it's the middle of August."

The bewildered drunk looked at him and said, "My God, my wife will kill me! I've never been *this* late before."

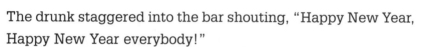

"I always wake up at the crack of ice."
— Joe E. Lewis (1902-1971), American comedian and actor

As a drunk staggered his way homeward he pondered the ways of concealing his condition from his wife. "I'll go home and read," he decided. "Whoever heard of a drunken man reading a book?"

Later his wife heard a noise in the library and went to investigate. "What in the world are you doing in there?" she asks.

"Reading, my luv," he replied.

"You idiot!" she says as she looks in the library door. "Shut up that suitcase and come to bed!"

> "It's a great advantage not to drink among hard-drinking people. You can hold your tongue and, moreover, you can time any little irregularity of your own so that everybody else is so blind that they don't see or care."
>
> – Francis Scott Key Fitzgerald (1896-1940),
> American writer

You know you like to drink when:

➤ You stop doing things in halves and do them in fifths.

➤ You return from lunch and you're so loaded they make you use the freight elevator.

➤ Your doctor's worried that you have too little blood in your alcohol stream.

➤ You buy a bottle of whisky for your cold, and in no time at all it's gone. Not the cold—the whisky.

➤ You go to an orthopedist to immobilize your elbow. Even though you're not drinking, every time you bend it, your mouth snaps open.

➤ If it wasn't for the pretzels you'd be entirely on a liquid diet.

➤ You spend so much time in bars you're developing rheumatism from picking up wet change.

➤ Instead of getting sober from drinking your Bloody Marys mixed with carrot juice, you see better.

➤ The only exercise you ever get is hiccupping.

➤ You frequent so many bars, your suits aren't dry-cleaned—they're distilled.

➤ On your birthday, with just one breath you light all the candles on your birthday cake.

Q: What's Irish and stays out all night?
A: Paddy O'Furniture.

A **giant wrestler sits down** at a bar next to a dwarf about three feet tall. After watching the little fellow belt down a dozen martinis, the wrestler asks, "Where do you put them, buddy?" The dwarf turns and pinches the wrestler on the cheek. "Hey!" The wrestler says. "Don't do that." The dwarf pinches him again. "Do it again and I'll flatten you."

A third time the dwarf pinches the wrestler's cheek. The wrestler picks up the dwarf, hits him with a dozen karate chops, drop-kicks him in the groin, bouncing him off the wall, and sums up the beating with three more kicks in the groin. Nothing seems to affect the dwarf, who shakes his head and then proceeds to beat up the wrestler. He bounces the giant off the floor like a rubber ball. Finished, he drapes the wrestler over the barstool.

Ten minutes later, the wrestler comes to. He walks over to the midget, who prepares for action. The wrestler shakes off the thought of doing battle. "Look," he says, "I don't want to fight. I just want to know why you didn't die when I kicked you in the groin. It must be painful."

The dwarf says, "I'm from another planet. We have nothing under our belts."

"Well, how do you have sex?"

The dwarf leans over and pinches the wrestler again!

An inmate of the alcoholic ward fingered his flashlight lovingly. "If I turn this beam straight up in the air," he said to his roommate, "I'll bet you a million dollars you can't climb up it." "I'm wise to your tricks," sneered his friend. "I'd get half way up and you'd turn it off."

> **"NECTAR. n. A drink served in banquets of the Olympian deities. The secret of its preparation is lost, but the modern Kentuckians believe that they come pretty near to a knowledge of its chief ingredient."**
>
> — Ambrose Bierce, American journalist and short-story writer

A man walked into a bar and slumped down on an empty bar stool. Looking up, he said to the bartender, "I just lost my job, my wife, my car, and my house. Gimme a drink."

The bartender replied, "Listen buddy, if you are drinking to forget, could you pay first?"

ANOTHER ROUND!

> ## "Those who drink beer will think beer."
> — Washington Irving (1788-1859), American short-story writer and essayist

> ## "Either you're drunk or your braces are lopsided."
> — W.C. Fields

> ## "I drink when I have occasion, and sometimes when I have no occasion."
> — Miguel de Cervantes (1547-1616), Spanish writer

It was closing time at the saloon and the same four drunks were sprawled along the bar. The bartender gathered them up and deposited them in a taxi outside. "Here's ten bucks," he said to the driver. "Drop the guy on the left at 12 Main Street, the one next to him at 40 Elm Street, and the one next to him at 130 Fifth Street. The fourth guy goes all the way over to the domestic apartments."

The taxi drives off, but comes back again inside of ten minutes. "Hey, bartender," the driver cries. "Will you please come over and sort these guys out for me again? I hit a bump on Park Avenue."

Upon taking a seat at the bar, the exec noticed that each stool had a number painted on it. Sitting next to him was a rather depressed looking gentleman and an attractive blonde who was obviously enjoying herself. The new-comer turned toward the unhappy fellow and asked if he knew the purpose of the numbers.

"Sure," answered the chap. "Every half hour, the bartender spins a wheel and whoever has the winning seat gets to go upstairs for the wild sex orgy they have up there."

"That's terrific!" exclaimed the surprised customer. "Have you won?"

"Not yet," shot back the man, "but my date has—four times in a row."

~~~~

A drunk was sitting at the bar adjacent to a man with his wife. Suddenly the drunk came fourth with a resounding burp. "How dare you belch before my wife!" thundered the husband. With that the drunk unsteadily got to his feet and with a graceful bow said, "A thousand pardons, sir...I did not know it was the madam's turn."

> ## "Real friends are those who, when you've made a fool of yourself, don't feel you've done a permanent job."
>
> —Anonymous

> **"A college education doesn't make fools; it just develops them."**
>
> —Anonymous

> **"The only man who sticks closer to you in adversity than a friend is a creditor."**
>
> —Anonymous

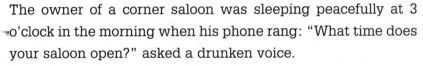

The owner of a corner saloon was sleeping peacefully at 3 o'clock in the morning when his phone rang: "What time does your saloon open?" asked a drunken voice.

"Eleven o'clock," said the saloon-keeper, and slammed down the phone.

A minute later the bell rang again. The same voice asked, "What time did you say your saloon opened?"

"Eleven o'clock, damn it," roared the proprietor, "and you can't get in a minute before!"

"Who wants to get in?" said a very hurt voice. "I want to get out!"

Two guys are sitting in a bar, bragging about all the people they know. The bartender gets fed up and says he knows the governor. The bartender says, "I'm Joe Doaks, and everyone knows Joe Doaks." The two men bet him $100. They all get on separate phone extensions, and the bartender calls the governor, talks to him like they're old friends. The two men pay up and are quiet for awhile.

After a couple more drinks, they are bragging again. The bartender gets mad and tells them he knows the President of the United States. The bartender says, "I'm Joe Doaks, and everyone knows Joe Doaks." The two men now bet him $1,000. Again, they all get on the phone; the bartender calls the White House and is transferred immediately to the Oval Office. The bartender chats with the president about old times. The two men pay up and are quiet again.

After a few more drinks the two men are bragging yet again. The bartender finally has had enough and blurts out that he knows the pope. The bartender says, "I'm Joe Doaks, and everyone knows Joe Doaks." The two men, shocked, call his bluff and bet the bartender $10,000. All three agree to fly to Rome. Once there, they walk across St. Peter's Square. When they get to three large doors, the bartender tells them only he can go in, as the pope doesn't see just anybody. He enters and is gone for a long time. Finally, he appears on a second-floor porch and waves. Then a little old man wearing a white robe and a beanie appears, and he too waves. The two men aren't sure if that's the pope, so they ask a group of Italians standing around who that old man is.

One of them replies, "I don't know, but the other guy is Joe Doaks."

—Jack R. Wallets, TX

As the delivery man lugged in the shiny new bar for her husband's den, his wife turned and said, "Howard, your life-support system has arrived."

~~~

Morseley ran into the tavern and said to Barney the bartender, "I just swallowed a live bullet. What should I do?"

"Eat a lot of radishes," calmly replied Barney, "and have a long conversation with your mother-in law."

"Living on a budget is the same as living beyond your means, except that you have a record of it."

—Anonymous

"Let us eat and drink for tomorrow we die."

— The New Testament

> **"Life is a jigsaw puzzle with most of the pieces missing."**
>
> —Anonymous

> **"If the opposite of 'pro' is 'con,' then what is the opposite of progress?"**
>
> —Anonymous

Not feeling well, Stan called on his family doctor who looked him over. The doctor prescribed pills to be taken at bedtime and whisky in a small glass to be taken after each meal for his stomach's sake. Four days later, Stan again called on his doctor, stating that he was feeling no better. "Have you taken the medicine exactly as I have instructed?" the doctor inquired.

"Well, doctor," replied Stan, "I may be a bit behind with the pills, but I'm six weeks ahead with the whisky."

> **"There are two reasons for drinking; one is, when you are thirsty, to cure it; the other, when you are not thirsty, to prevent it. Prevention is better than cure."**
>
> — T.L. Peacock, *Melincourt*

A man strolled into a bar and ordered a martini. Before drinking the martini, the customer removed the olive and dropped it into a small glass jar. He then ordered two more martinis and followed the same procedure. All in all, he ordered 12 martinis, dropped each olive into his glass jar, downed the drink.

When eventually he staggered out of the place, a near-by customer turned to the bartender and said, "That's the strangest thing I've ever seen."

"Nothing strange at all," explained the bartender. "His wife just sent him out for a jar of olives."

> ## "Talk is cheap because supply exceeds demand."
> —Anonymous

> ## "We can be absolutely certain only about things we do not understand."
> —Anonymous

"Abstinence," said Father clearly, "is a wonderful thing, Bragan!"

"Sure and it is, Father," said Bragan, "if practiced in moderation."

The old man was having trouble with his eyes so he decided to see a doctor. "Well, sir," said the doctor, "heavy drinking has brought this on. Now you have to stop drinking or you will go blind. You must choose between the two."

"Well, doc," replied the man, "I am an old man and think I've just about seen everything."

> ## "To buy very good wine nowadays requires only money. To serve it to your guests is a sign of fatigue."
>
> — William F. Buckley, Jr., quoted by Ellen Peck in Harper's Bazaar
>
>
>
> ## "Despite inflation, a penny is still a fair price for the thoughts of many people."
>
> —Anonymous

Clancy rushed into Sullivan's tavern and cried, "Timmy, me bucko, give me three whiskeys before the trouble starts."

Sullivan gave him the drinks and said, "Now then, Mike, what's the trouble and when does it start?"

"Right now," Clancy assured him. "I ain't got a penny in me pocket!"

CHEERS!

An exhausted business executive gratefully climbed into his bed in a Washington hotel at midnight, looking forward to a solid nine-hour sleep. At 2 a.m., however, a loud banging on his door awakened him. It was a semi-coherent drunk, angrily declaring, "Thish ish my room. Get out!" It took the executive twenty minutes to get back to sleep. Once more he was awakened by the same drunk an hour later, who still claimed the room was his.

When the drunk woke him up a third time, the executive literally blew his top, but this time the drunk got in the first words. "So it's you again!" He screamed. "Damn it, are you occupying every room in this hotel?!"

> ## "He who drinks a little too much drinks much too much."
>
> — Proverb
>
> ---
>
> ## "Advice after injury is like medicine after death."
>
> —Anonymous

Bar signs

- Drink here. Four out of five accidents occur at home.
- If you drink to forget, please pay in advance.
- Not responsible for anything said after three beers.
- Please don't drink on an empty wallet.
- If you must drive your husband to drink, drive him here.
- Please do not drink more than you can walk out with.

The fellow walked into a bar he had never been in before and ordered a drink. He then asked the bartender if he enjoyed dumb-jock jokes. The beefy attendant leaned over the bar and fixed a withering glare on his customer. "Listen, buddy," he growled. "See these two big guys on the left? They're professional football players. And that huge guy in the corner is a champion weightlifter. And I lettered in three sports at Notre Dame." Now, are you absolutely positive you want to go ahead and tell your dumb-jock joke here?"

"Nah, guess not," the man replied. "I wouldn't want to have to explain it five times."

"Man who beef too much find himself in stew."

—Anonymous

A drunk was hanging on to a lamppost for dear life when an old lady walked by and said, "Why don't you take a bus home?" The drunk said, "My wife would never let me keep it!"

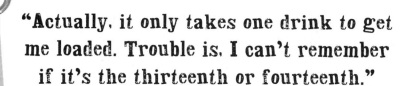

"Actually, it only takes one drink to get me loaded. Trouble is, I can't remember if it's the thirteenth or fourteenth."

—George Burns

Identical twins sauntered into a bar and laughed as one of the customers started to gawk at them. One of the twins said, "Don't worry, the booze hasn't affected you. We're twins." The man said, "No kidding, all four of you?"

"A woman drove me to drink and I didn't even have the decency to thank her."

—W. C. Fields

A wine-soaked gentleman of the river section staggered into a swanky Kansas City hotel bar and planked down a thin dime.

"Gimme a ten-cent whiskey."

"I'm sorry, sir," said the polite bartender, "but we do not serve ten-cent whiskey."

"Then gimme my dime back. I don't want none of that nickel stuff. It makes me sick."

~~~

HE: "You remind me of a can of beer in my neighbor's icebox."

SHE: "Just what do you mean?"

HE: "You're so cold and distant."

> "Give a strong drink unto him that is ready to perish, and wine unto those that be of heavy hearts. Let him drink, and forget his poverty, and remember his misery no more."
>
> — "Proverbs" 31:6-7

"UH OH, HERE COME THE
SUMMER PEOPLE."

> **"Of my merit On that pint you yourself may judge; All is, I never drink no spirit, Nor I haint never signed no pledge."**
>
> — James Russell Lowell (1819-1891)

> **"I drink to the general joy o' the whole table."**
>
> — William Shakespeare, *Macbeth* (ca. 1603-1606)

A man walked into a bar and sat down. There didn't seem to be a bartender. After a few moments, from the door at the back of the bar, a horse came out. Tying an apron around his waist, the horse asked the man if he wanted a drink. The man stared. The horse asked, "Why are you staring? Didn't you ever see a horse before?"

The man answered, "Well, I didn't think the cow would ever sell the place!"

Borderline
☞
ZANY!

Clancy had sworn off drinking over his vacation and had clung to his decision stubbornly for weeks. He knew nevertheless, that the real crunch would come when he went back to work, for on his way home he would have to pass not one, not two, but five bars in rapid succession.

On his first day at work, he spent the whole day working up his will power. Finally, with perspiration bespangling his brow, he set off on that journey home. He passes the first two bars with a grim set to his jaw and without a sideward glance. At the third bar he looked at the windows longingly, but never slowed his step. At the fourth, he faltered, then forced himself on with an effort.

Finally, he was at the fifth, Joe's Bar, a favorite of his over many years. Inside were his friends. Inside was warmth, song, joy, camaraderie—all that gave life its special flavor. For long minutes, he stood there on the sidewalk, gazing at the doorway and filled with yearning. But then he gave himself a shake and remembered his resolution. With a supreme effort, he forced his muscles to his well and walked away.

He had gone half a block before it really sank in that he had beaten temptation; he had actually passed five bars in a row—he had even passed Joe's Bar!

And in sheer ecstasy, he went back to Joe's Bar for a drink to celebrate the victory.

> **"Busy, curious, thirst fly. Drink with me, and Drink as I."**
>
> — William Oldys (1696-1761)

> **"There never was a cause yet, right or wrong, that ever wanted an advocate to defend it."**
>
> —Anonymous

Two men met at a bar and had a great evening together. They promised to meet at the same bar a year from that day. One of the men returned at the exact moment and found the other sitting, waiting for him. "When did you get here?" the man asked.

The other said, "Who left?"

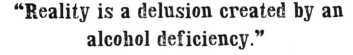

> **"Reality is a delusion created by an alcohol deficiency."**
>
> —Anonymous

Two sailors get off a ship and head for the nearest bar. Each one orders two whiskeys and immediately downs them. They then order two more whiskeys apiece. One of them picks up one of his drinks, and, turning to the other man says, "Cheers!"

The other man turns to the first and says, "Hey, did you come here to shoot the bull, or did you come here to drink?"

> "...with you, talk with you, walk with you, and so following; but I will not eat with you, drink with you, nor pray with you. What news on the Rialto?"
>
> — William Shakespeare,
> *The Merchant of Venice* (1594-1597)
>
> ———
>
> "An evil mind is a constant solace."
>
> —Anonymous

Two fellows decided to go ice fishing. They began chipping away at the ice. Shortly, they heard a voice yelling, "There's no fish here." This happened two or three times. Finally, a guy came up to them and said, "I told you there are no fish here. This rink is closed!"

—CAROL TATUM, CA

ANOTHER ROUND!

A group from the United Nations is having a drink at a near-by New York bar. One of the delegates says to the group, "Pardon me, but what's your opinion of the food shortage?"

The delegate from Quebec says, "What shortage?"

The delegate from Moscow says, "What's food?"

The delegate from Havana says, "What's an opinion?"

And the delegate from New York says, "What's 'pardon me'?"

> ## "I told my wife that a husband is like a fine wine; he gets better with age. The next day, she locked me in the cellar."
>
> — Anonymous
>
>
>
> ## "Our style betrays us."
>
> —Anonymous

A grasshopper walks into a bar and sits down. The bartender notices him and says, "You know something, buddy, they named a drink after you."

"No kidding," says the grasshopper. "They've got a drink named Bruce?"

An enterprising bartender saved his money and finally bought a saloon in an old western town. Opening night was great, with wall to wall people. All of a sudden an old prospector ran in and yelled, "Head for the hills everybody, big John's comin'!"

Instantly everybody headed for the door. As the last patron was running out the door he asked the new owner, "Hey man, ain't you comin'?"

"Hell no," he answered. "I own this place. I just can't walk out and leave everything," he answered.

"Hey man," said the customer. "You'll be sorry. Big John's comin'." After a time heavy footsteps were heard outside and suddenly the swinging doors crashed open and an eight-foot, 400 pound creature with long shaggy hair and bright red eyes appeared in the doorway. The stranger lumbered up to the bar and the bartender walked down wide eyed and trembling. "Ya-ya-yes si-si-sir, ca-ca-can I, I ge-ge-get you something?"

"Yeah," roared the monster! "Whiskey!!"

The bartender set the bottle on the bar and reached for a glass, but the huge man grabbed the bottle, bit the top off it, and downed the contents in one gulp. "Oh lord," asked the terrified bartender, "ca-ca-can I get ya another one?"

"Hell no," roared the giant! "I ain't got time! Didn't ya hear? Big John's comin!!"

—RUSSELL LEWELLEN, BIRMINGHAM, AL

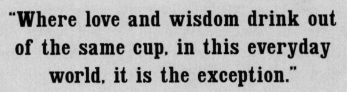

> "Where love and wisdom drink out of the same cup, in this everyday world, it is the exception."
>
> — Madame Necker

> "Eat, drink, and be merry, for tomorrow we diet."
>
> — Anonymous

Did you hear about the man that staggered up to the parking meter and exclaimed, "My God! I've lost 120 pounds!"

A cop pulls over a drunk who ran a red light and asked, "Didn't you see that red light back there?"
The drunk replied, "Yeah, but I didn't see you."

Shortly after purchasing a mynah bird, a bar owner named Jack went on vacation. While he was away his friends sat at the bar and taught the bird to say a phrase to their advantage. When Jack returned, the bird repeated over and over, "Buy the house a drink, Jack!"

~~~~~

A hamburger walks into a bar, and the bartender says, "I'm sorry, but we don't serve food here…"

"I drank at every vine./The last was like the first. /I came upon no wine./ So wonderful as thirst."
— Edna St. Vincent Millay, "Feast," *The Ballad of the Harp-Weaver*

"Success is not so much what you are, but rather what you appear to be."
—Anonymous

"It takes time to be a success, but time is all it takes."
—Anonymous

Hymie Lipshitz's **10** laws of bartending:

➤ No one orders a Brandy Alexander when you're slow.
➤ The person who wins the fight over the check is the worst tipper.
➤ Last call is always given twice.
➤ No one has ever been drunk before.
➤ All customers can get you a better job.
➤ No one's at a bar when their spouse calls.
➤ All customers know the owner better than you.
➤ Anyone who wants to buy you a drink never offers you the money.
➤ Everyone leaves their proof of age at home.
➤ The owner always has relatives that can bartend.

What's the difference between a stagecoach driver and a bartender?

A stagecoach driver only has to look at four assholes a day!

Two men were staggering down the street when one said, "It takes me an hour or so to get ashleep when I go home."

The other replied, "Thash funny. I always fall ashleep ash shoon ash I hit da bed."

"Sho do I," said the first. "My trouble esh hitting the bed."

Doctor to patient: "Please stretch out your hands."

The man did and they trembled violently.

"Good heavens, how much do you drink?" asked the doctor.

"Very little," said the patient. "I spill most of it."

"I had a bad cold and a fellow told me that the best thing to do for it was to drink a quart of whiskey and go home to bed. On the way home another fellow told me the same thing. That made a half gallon."

— Mark Twain

"His shortcoming is his long staying."

—Anonymous

A bartender told a man that he had had enough. The man replied, "I just lost my wife, buddy!"

The bartender said, "It must be hard losing a wife."

The man said, "It was almost impossible."

HAVE ANOTHER!

> **"Anything which parents have not learned from experience they can now learn from their children."**
>
> —Anonymous

> **"Drink is your enemy—love your enemies."**
>
> — W.C. Fields

I told her I'd by home by three
I know she'll be up waiting for me,
If I call her now and talk real nice,
I might calm her down and break the ice.
But she'll lock the door and bolt the latch,
And I'll be forced to ring the bell,
Then she'll break loose with all hell.
Well I'd better leave real soon
After all, it's my honeymoon.

~~~~~

The man asked a policeman, "Shay which ish the other shide o the shtreet?"

"Why over there, of course," came the reply

"Shtrange. I was just over there an a gentlemen shaid it wuz over here."

rib tickler!

A man goes into a bar with a dog and the two of them sit down facing the bartender. Seeing the dog, the bartender says, "Sorry fellas, we don't serve dogs in here."

"But this dog talks, bartender. Is that okay?"

"C'mon mister," laughs the bartender. "Who ever heard of a talking dog?"

"No, really, he can talk. I'll show you." Turning to the dog, he asks, "Sparky, what goes on top of a house?"

"Roof!" barks the dog.

"Get outta here," snarls the bartender. "Any dog'd do that."

"Okay, okay," replies the man, "let me ask him another. Sparky, what does sandpaper feel like?"

"Ruff!" answers the dog.

"Why you jerk," yells the bartender, "get him outta here before I throw you out!"

"Wait, one more try," pleads the man. Grimly the bartender nods his assent.

"Who's the greatest Yankee outfielder of all time!"

"Ruth!" barks Sparky without hesitation.

"That's it, you two, you're outta here," yells the bartender picking up the two and tossing them out the front door. The two land in the gutter face down, and the dog is the first to recover his senses. Sparky looks up at the man quizzically. "Di Maggio?"

> "A bottle of wine contains more philosophy than all the books in the world."
>
> — Louis Pasteur

Here's a ZINGER!

> "Conscience gets a lot of credit that belongs to cold feet."
>
> —Anonymous

Sitting at a bar, looking glum, a guy mutters, "Problems, always problems."

"What problems?" asks the bartender.

"My wife and I just booked a two-week vacation in the Caribbean," explains the man. "One kid is at Harvard and the other at Yale. We just put in a new swimming pool…"

"That sounds pretty good to me," interrupts the barkeep.

"Not really," replies the guy. "I only make $200 a week."

~~~

Two peanuts walked into a bar, and one was a salted…

A Swede walked into a saloon and asked for a drink of squirrel whiskey. The bartender said, "I haven't any squirrel whiskey, but I do have some Old Crow."

The Swede said, "I didn't want to fly. I yust wanted to yump around a little!"

> **"Abstainer: a weak person who yields to the temptation of denying himself a pleasure."**
>
> — Ambrose Bierce
>
>
>
> **"A drink a day keeps the shrink away."**
>
> — Edward Abbey

A couple had been imbibing heavily for some time in a cocktail lounge. Suddenly, the waiter rushed over and said to the woman, "Madam, your husband has just slipped under the table."

"No," replied the woman, with aplomb. "My husband has just walked in the door."

> **"The wretchedness of being rich is that you live with rich people. To suppose, as we all suppose, that we could be rich and not behave as the rich behave, is like supposing that we could drink water all day and stay sober."**
>
> — Logan Pearsall Smith (1865-1946),
> American essayist and editor

The drunk was fumbling at his keyhole in the early hours of the morning. A policeman saw his difficulty and came to the rescue. "Can I help you to find the keyhole, sir?" he asked.

"Thash all right, orafficer," said the drunk cheerily, "you just hol the housh still and I can manage."

~~~~

The sweet young thing was sitting at the cocktail party with a new conquest. "My, but you're beautiful," he said. "Let me get a couple of drinks and we'll sit and talk."

"None for me," she called after him. "I never drink."

However, he soon returned with two drinks. "Are you sure you wouldn't like to try, just this once?" he asked.

"Well, just this once," She took a sip.

A lecturer was annoyed by a drunken man in the audience who insisted upon rising and asking silly questions. "Sit down, you ass!" cried a second man in the audience, jumping up. "Sit down, the both of you!" shouted a third, "You're both asses." Visibly upset, the lecturer said, "There seem to be plenty of asses here tonight but for heaven's sake, let's hear one at a time." Whereupon the first man cried, "Well, you go on, then," and resumed his seat.

Downright WACKY!

A **skunk, a giraffe, and a deer** walked into a bar one evening and ordered three whiskeys. When the drinks arrived, the trio belted them down, and ordered three more. The bartender again poured out the drinks. Again the three quaffed them quickly. Another round was ordered and, with some trepidation since he saw no wallets on any of the three, the bartender served up the order.

After the three animals finished their drinks, they started for the door. "Wait a minute, you three," shouted the bartender. "How about paying me?"

"I can't," said the skunk, "I only have a scent."

"I can't," seconded the deer, "I had a buck last week, but I'm expecting a little doe."

"Well," sighed the giraffe as he walked back toward the bartender. "I guess that means the high balls are on me."

> ### "Originality is the art of concealing your sources."
>
> —Anonymous
>
>
>
> ### "What's one man's poison, signor, is another's meat or drink."
>
> — Beaumont and Fletcher

The man asked the bartender to suggest a drink. "Rum flip," said the bartender. "It has sugar, milk and rum. The sugar gives you energy, the milk strength."

"What does the rum give you?"

"Ideas about what to do with the energy and strength."

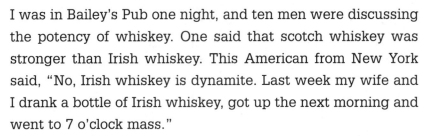

I was in Bailey's Pub one night, and ten men were discussing the potency of whiskey. One said that scotch whiskey was stronger than Irish whiskey. This American from New York said, "No, Irish whiskey is dynamite. Last week my wife and I drank a bottle of Irish whiskey, got up the next morning and went to 7 o'clock mass."

Murphy said, "What's unusual about that? Lots of us drink a bottle of Irish whiskey and go to mass the next day."

The American said, "I know, but we're Jewish."

JOHN: "Poor Calhoun's sufferin' from that old Irish disease called alcoholic rheumatism."

JACK: "What in the saints' names is alcoholic rheumatism?"

JOHN: "He gets stiff in all the joints!"

> ## "You can't be a real country unless you have a beer and an airline— it helps if you have some kind of a football team, or some nuclear weapons, but at the very least you need a beer."
>
> — Frank Zappa
>
>
>
> ## "Man thinks. God laughs."
>
> —Anonymous

A man was sitting in a bar when a young punk rocker came in. The punk rocker had purple hair and very colorful clothes on. The man gave him a strange look so the punk rocker said, "Hey man, haven't you ever done anything crazy?"

CHEERS!

"It was terrible," says the bartender to the cop. "Just as I was closing up, two elephants came in here and held me up."

"What did they look like?" asks the cop. "If they had big ears, they were African elephants, and if they had small ears, they would be from India."

"How the hell should I know what kind of ears they had? They were wearing stocking masks!"

~~~~~

One bar manager was forced to fire one of his waitresses. He says to the owner, "She keeps asking me what to do about the simplest problems...and it's getting embarrassing to keep saying I don't know."

> ## "Who builds upon the people, builds upon sand."
> —Anonymous

> ## "A man without a beer is like a doctor without a condominium, a lawyer without a tongue, the Yankees with a manager, my wife without a complaint..."
> —Norm, *Cheers*

Visiting a midtown bar, a man ordered a Manhattan. When it was placed before him, a sprig of parsley floated therein. "What's that thing in my Manhattan?" He demanded angrily. The quick-thinking bartender answered spryly. "That's Central Park."

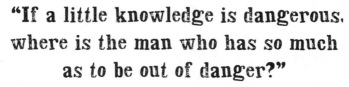

Here's a ZINGER!

"If a little knowledge is dangerous, where is the man who has so much as to be out of danger?"

—Anonymous

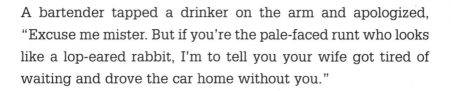

A bartender tapped a drinker on the arm and apologized, "Excuse me mister. But if you're the pale-faced runt who looks like a lop-eared rabbit, I'm to tell you your wife got tired of waiting and drove the car home without you."

A man noticed a sign on the window of a bar saying, "All the beer you can drink for one dollar. He went in and said, "That sounds like a good deal. I'll take two dollars' worth."

Whiskey's wisdoms :

➤ They never serve who only stand and drink.

➤ When intoxicated a Frenchman wants to dance; a German to sing; a Spaniard to gamble; an Englishman to boast; an Italian to eat; an Irishman to fight; and an American to make a speech.

➤ Show me a man who drinks prune juice and whiskey every day, and I'll show you a regular drunk.

The sun-baked cowboy swaggered into the saloon and through parched lips ordered the bartender to give his horse a bucket of his best whiskey. "And what'll you have, stranger?" asked the bartender.

"Nothin'," shot back the dusty cowboy, "I'm drivin'!"

~~~

Three young men purchased a tavern and were in the process of cleaning up prior to opening. One lad, of Irish descent, says to his partners, "Fellows, we have to recover these chairs and stools with a bright green material."

The second partner, of Scottish descent, chides in. "We must do it, but I think a nice, bright plaid would cheer the place up."

The third fellow, a former banker, looks up from his work and states, "Let's just cover them with buttocks so we can make some money!"

The bachelor, a poor tipper, walked into his favorite bar and ordered a drink. The new barmaid received a three-cent tip. When he returned the next evening, she thanked him for his "generosity" and told him she could tell his character from the way he tipped. "Tell me," he asked. "The way you put the three pennies in a row shows you're very neat," she said. "The first penny," she went on, "tells me you're frugal, the second penny tells me you're a bachelor, and the third penny tells me your father was a bachelor, too."

> **"I like good whiskey and good-looking women. I'm scared to death of being stone-cold sober...I'm a religious person."**
>
> — Jerry Lee Lewis

> **"Eat, drink, and be merry, for tomorrow they may cancel your VISA."**
>
> — Anonymous

> **"Experience is what you get when you expected something else."**
>
> —Anonymous

Two former classmates met after many years and stepped into the local bar to celebrate. After a bit of celebration, one said to the other, "Look at the time! Doesn't your wife raise hell when you stay out this late?"

"I'm not married," replied the friend.

"Not married!" exclaimed the first fellow. "Then why do you stay out late like this?"

> "Every year it takes less time to fly across the Atlantic, and more time to drive to the office."
>
> —Anonymous

> "The greatest thrill known to man isn't flying—it's landing."
>
> —Anonymous

The bartender, chatting with one of the regulars, said, "I hear that your wife has converted you to religion."

"Oh, yes," the fellow replied with a sigh. "I had no idea of what hell was until I married her."

HAVE ANOTHER!

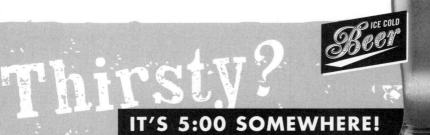

A seedy-looking character walked into Joe's bar one day and seated himself on a bar stool. Joe was about to ask him to leave when the guy said, "Gimme a scotch and soda, set up the bar and have one yourself."

"Gee, I guess I was mistaken about this one," thought Joe as he hurried to fill the order.

After the half-dozen other bar flies had thanked him, this character says, "Same thing again. Scotch and soda for me, set up the bar and have one yourself."

"Yes, sir," answered Joe. "This guy is really a sport."

After finishing his drink, the customer got off of the stool and started for the door. "Hey," called Joe, uncertainly, "Where ya going? You owe me twenty eight bucks!"

"I haven't got any money," the bum answered with a grin. "What!" screamed Joe and with that he threw the guy out on the street.

A week or two passed and one day who should come into the bar but the same guy who had fleeced Joe before. He jumped up on a bar stool and with a voice of authority said. "Gimme a scotch and soda and set up the bar!"

Joe stared at him balefully and said with a sneer. "What's the matter, don't I get one this time?"

"The hell with you," the bum replied, "You're too damn nasty when you're drinking!"

—RALPH W. FITZPATRICK, MA

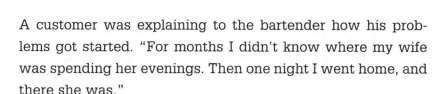

A customer was explaining to the bartender how his problems got started. "For months I didn't know where my wife was spending her evenings. Then one night I went home, and there she was."

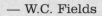

There were three men sitting at the bar after work.

"Let's have a drink to remind us of our bosses," the first one said.

"I'll have a beer and put a big head on it."

"Give me a whiskey sour," the second said, "reminds me of his sour disposition."

"Make mine a tequila sunrise," the third said, "and make sure the worm is dead."

> "Reminds me of my safari in Africa. Somebody forgot the corkscrew and for several days we had nothing to live on but food and water."
> — W.C. Fields

> "Love your enemy—it'll drive him nuts."
> —Anonymous

> "Science opens to us the book of nature; comedy, the book of human nature."
>
> —Anonymous

The Scotsman ordered a scotch and only tipped a nickel because he was thrifty.

The Russian ordered a vodka and only tipped a dime because he did not make much money in Siberia.

The Japanese tourist ordered a sake and tipped $100 because he had the yen to do it.

What is the difference between beer nuts and deer nuts?

Beer nuts are $1.49 and deer nuts are under a buck.

> "Tell the truth and run."
>
> —Anonymous

> ## "A bachelor never makes the same mistake once."
> —Anonymous
>
>
>
> ## "Writing about art is like dancing about architecture."
> —Anonymous

A bartender was literally running around in circles – serving drinks at an oval-shaped bar – when he noticed that his customers had fallen unusually quiet. Absolutely silent, as a matter of fact. Following their eyes, he saw that they were staring at one of their number – a fellow who had gotten up on one side of the oval bar, walked calmly up the wall and across the ceiling, down the other wall, and out the door.

An amazed customer finally found his voice.

"What do you think of that?" He exclaimed, as the drinker disappeared down the street.

"Yeah," said the bartender, polishing a glass, "he never says goodnight."

A man stumbles up to the only other patron in a bar and asks if he could buy him a drink. "Why of course," comes the reply.

The first man then asks, "Where are you from?" "I'm from Ireland," replies the second man.

The first man responds, "You don't say. I'm from Ireland too! Let's have another round to Ireland."

"Of course," replies the second man.

Curious, the first man then asks, "Where in Ireland are you from?" "Dublin," comes the reply. "I can't believe it," says the first man. "I'm from Dublin too! Let's have another drink to Dublin." "Of course," replies the second man.

Curiosity again strikes and the first man asks, "What school did you go to?" "Saint Mary's," replies the second man. "I graduated in '62." "This is unbelievable," the first man says. "I went to Saint Mary's and I graduated in '62, too!"

About that time, in comes one of the regulars and sits down at the bar. "What's been going on?" He asks the bartender. "Nothing much," replies the bartender. "The O'Malley twins are drunk again."

—DENICE SCHENCK, POSTAL EMPLOYEE, LIBERTY CORNER, NJ

"Three highballs, and I think I'm St. Francis of Assisi."

— Dorothy Parker, *Just a Little One*

A panda walks into a bar, sits down and orders a sandwich. He eats the sandwich, pulls out a gun and shoots the waiter dead. As the panda stands up to go, the bartender shouts, "Hey! Where are you going? You just shot my waiter and you didn't pay for your sandwich." The panda yells back at the bartender, "Hey man, I'm a panda! Look it up!"

The bartender opens his dictionary and sees the following definition for panda: a tree-dwelling marsupial of Asian origin, characterized by distinct black and white coloring. Eats shoots and leaves.

> ## "Beer is proof that God loves and wants us to be happy."
>
> —Benjamin Franklin
>
>
>
> ## "Time is never wasted when you're wasted at the time."
>
> —Catherine Zandonella

Customer to bartender: "Hey, gimme a horse's neck."

Second customer: "I'll have a horses tail. There's no use killing two horses."

ANOTHER ROUND!

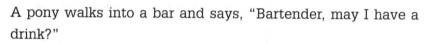

> "To be always intending to live a new life, but never find time to set about it—this is as if a man should put off eating and drinking from one day to another till he be starved and destroyed."
>
> — Sir Walter Scott

A pony walks into a bar and says, "Bartender, may I have a drink?"

The bartender says, "Speak up, I can't hear you."

"May I please have a cocktail?"

"Look, if you don't speak up, I will not serve you."

"I'm awfully sorry! I'm just a little horse."

~~~~

Mr. Smith shook his head. "No, sir," he said, "I cannot accept your offer of a cocktail at this hour for three reasons. First, I promised my wife never to drink during the business day. Second, liquor before lunch incapacitates me for work all afternoon. Third, I had three just before you came in."

"However," continued Smith hurriedly, "I do not want to injure the feelings of a distinguished New York colleague. You might order me two double martinis."

The man walked into Malloy's Bar and ordered drinks for everybody including the bartender. He then confessed he didn't have a dime. The bartender gave him two shiners and heaved him out. The next day he repeated the same stunt and again the bartender worked him over and tossed him out. Back he came for the third night and again ordered drinks for everyone.

"Me too?" asked the bartender.

"Certainly not," said the man. "One drink and you're a raving maniac."

> **"Alcohol is an admirable commodity which enables parliament to do things at eleven at night that no sane person would do at eleven in the morning."**
>
> — George Bernard Shaw

> **"Any fool can make a rule, and every fool will mind it."**
>
> —Anonymous

A **magician was working** on a cruise ship in the Caribbean. The audience would be different each week, so the magician allowed himself to do the same tricks over and over again.

There was only one problem. The captain's parrot saw the shows each week and began to understand how the magician did every trick. Once he understood he started shouting in the middle of the show:

"Look, it's not the same hat."

"Look, he is hiding the flowers under the table."

"Hey, why are all the cards the ace of spades?"

The magician was furious but couldn't do anything; it was, after all, the captain's parrot.

One day the ship had an accident and sank. The magician found himself on a piece of wood in the middle of the ocean with the parrot, of course. They stared at each other with hate, but did not utter a word. This went on for a day and another and another. After a week the parrot said: "Okay, I give up. Where's the boat?"

A man tied his horse to a post and went into a saloon for a few drinks. When he went back outside the horse had been painted green. He was very angry and stormed back into the saloon demanding to know who had done it. A seven-foot-tall, 500-pound man responded, "I did. What about it?"

The owner of the horse replied, "I just wanted to let you know that the first coat is dry."

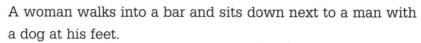

A woman walks into a bar and sits down next to a man with a dog at his feet.

"Does your dog bite?" she asks.

"No," is the reply.

A few moments later the dog bites her leg.

"I thought you said your dog doesn't bite!" the woman shrieks indignantly.

"He doesn't. That's not my dog."

A man leaves the bar. Outside he sees a nun. He walks over to her and slaps her in the face. Then he punches her in the stomach and knocks her down. He proceeds to kick her several times and when he's done he bends down to her and says, "Not so tough tonight, are you, Batman?"

> **"A hobby is hard work you wouldn't do for a living."**
> —Anonymous
>
>
>
> **"The beginning is easy: what happens next is much harder."**
> —Anonymous

"And why is that loafer McGee in the hospital again?" demanded the foreman.

"It's drunk he was again, I'm thinking."

"Positively not, sir," came McGee's wife to the rescue. "Twas a slight miscalculation McGee must've been making. He comes down the ladder just as careful as you please about five minutes after some scurvy blackguard took the damn ladder away."

> ## "There are several reasons for drinking. And one has just entered my head: If a man cannot drink when he's living, How the hell can he drink when he's dead?"
>
> — Anonymous
>
>
>
> ## "All sins cast long shadows."
>
> —Anonymous

MOTHER: "After all, he's only a boy, and boys will sow their wild oats."

FATHER: "Yes, but I wish he wouldn't sow so much rye with it."

CHEERS!

> ## "Things could be worse. Suppose your errors were counted and published every day, like those of a baseball player."
>
> —Anonymous

> ## "Originality is the art of concealing your sources."
>
> —Anonymous

McGee, returning from a trip to Ireland, was stopped by customs officials. He declared that the only thing he had with him was a bottle of water. "What kind of water?" asked the official.

"Sure, it's a bottle of holy water," said McGee.

The inspector had had experience with bottles before. He snatched this one out of the old man's hand, pulled open the cork and got a whiff of the contents. "It's whiskey," he declared triumphantly.

McGee rolled his eyes toward heaven and murmured in reverent tones, "Glory be to God! It's a miracle!"

Pat O'Flaherty, very palpably not a prohibitionist, was arrested in Arizona, charged with selling liquor in violation of the prohibition law. But Pat had an impregnable defense. His counsel, in addressing the jury, said: "Your honor, gentlemen of the jury, look at the defendant." A dramatic pause, then: "Now, gentlemen of the jury, do you honestly think that if the defendant had a quart of whiskey he would sell it?"

The verdict, reached in one minute, was not guilty.

—BETTY GADE, MI

> ## "If the student fails to learn the teacher fails to teach."
>
> —Anonymous

What happens when you step on a grape?
It lets out a little wine.

~~~

The fellow who had imbibed too freely stumbled along the street, bumped into a trashcan, bounced off a light pole and fell flat onto the sidewalk. "If I were in your condition," said a lady passing by, "I'd shoot myself."

"Lady," mumbled the fellow, "if you were in my condition, you'd miss."

> "**Now go, cat, go! But don't you step on my blue suede shoes. You can do anything but lay off my blue suede shoes. You can steal my car, drink my liquor from an old fruit jar. You can do anything you want to do. But don't you step on my blue suede shoes.**"
>
> — "Blue Suede Shoes"

Returning from a trip to Europe, Mark Twain became annoyed as a customs official rummaged through his baggage.

"My good friend," the author exclaimed, "you don't have to mix up all my things. There are only clothes in there—nothing but clothes."

But the suspicious fellow kept rooting around until he hit upon something hard. He pulled out a quart of the finest-quality bourbon.

"You call this just clothes?" cried the official.

"Sure thing," Twain replied. "That is my nightcap."

> **"Never put off until tomorrow what you can get someone else to do."**
>
> —Anonymous
>
>
>
> **"Nothing is impossible...if you don't have to do it yourself."**
>
> —Anonymous

An obviously successful businessman went into a hotel cocktail lounge early in the evening and commended to partake of double martinis. This went on for about two hours. A little later this lovely young woman came into the bar and sat close to him and started to do a little drinking. They ignored each other even though they were sitting two barstools apart. In trying to make casual conversation with the lady, he said, "About another drink and I'll be able to feel it."

She promptly said, "One more drink and I think I'll let you!"

—WILLIAM C. BRADSHAW, CA

Lincoln once replied to a prohibitionist's complaint that General Grant was overly fond of his bottle.

"Find out the brand of whiskey the general uses." Lincoln said. 'I would like to furnish the same brand to my other generals."

A **drunk walks into a bar** and sits down. In front of each stool he sees three darts. He calls the bartender over and says, "Hey! What are these darts here for?" The bartender says, "Well, you take the darts and throw them at the dart board behind the bar here, and anybody that gets three bull's-eye in a row wins a prize."

"Oh," says the drunk, stifling a burp, "all right." He picks up a dart and, weaving from side to side, hurls it. Clutching the bar at the last moment just in time to prevent himself from falling off the stool. Amazingly the dart lands firmly in the center of the bull's-eye.

He picks up the second dart, and with one hand on the bar steadying himself as best he can, he throws it. With his follow-through, he collapses onto the bar, his head hitting the wood with a resounding thump. Incredibly, though, the dart lodges itself right next to the other one. Another perfect bull's-eye.

The drunk then pushes himself up off the bar, picks up the third dart, and takes careful aim with two eyes that are looking in different directions. As he throws the last dart he falls backward off the stool and lands in a heap on the floor. But miraculously the dart lands once again in the bull's-eye.

As he stands up and wobbles over to the bar the drunk says loudly, "I want a prize! I want a prize!"

The bartender, astounded says to him, "Okay, buddy, okay. You'll get your prize. Just hang on a minute." As he turns around the bartender thinks to himself. "What am I going to do? Nobody has every won before. What am I going to give this guy?" Looking around the bar; he sees an old aquarium in the corner. He goes over, rolls up his sleeve, reaches into the water, and pulls out a nice, medium-size turtle. He goes back behind the bar and walks up to the drunk. "Okay, pal," he says, "here's your prize!"

The drunk's bloodshot eyes light up for an instant and he says, "Thanks a lot!" He then takes the turtle and staggers out of the bar.

A couple of weeks pass and then one day the same drunk stumbles back into the bar. He sits down at the same stool and calls out to the bartender, "I wanna try for a prize! I wanna try for a prize!"

The bartender walks over and says, "All right, buddy, go ahead."

The drunk then manages to repeat his previous performance with the one difference being that this time he manages to fall off the bar stool after every shot. However, he does make the three bull's-eyes.

"I want a prize!" He shouts. "I want a prize!" The bartender is totally flabbergasted. He says to the drunk, "I can't believe it! Nobody has ever done this before, and you've done it twice in a row!"

The drunk says, "Well, give my —gulp! P-p-prize."

The bartender says, "To tell you the truth, buddy, I just don't know what to give you. What did I give you last time?"

The drunk belches, smiles dreamily, and says, "Roast beef on a hard roll."

John was doing his best to fit his key into the lock, singing a happy song meanwhile. After awhile a head looked out of a window above. "Go away, you fool!" cried the man upstairs. "You're trying to get in the wrong house."

"Fool yourself!" shouted John, staggering below. "You're looking out of the wrong window!"

And then there was the slightly disoriented customer who decided to switch drinks: having had a few White Clouds, he now ordered a Blue Cloud. The bartender, remembering what he had been drinking, served him another White Cloud. When this met with the customer's indignant response, "I said blue!," the bartender casually removed the sip stick and stirred gently with a fountain pen.

—THOMAS SAVANESE, BERGEN BARTENDERS SCHOOL, LINDERHURST, NJ

> "Drink today, and drown all sorrow; You shall perhaps not do it tomorrow; Best, while you have it, use your breath; There is no drinking after death."
>
> — John Fletcher, "The Bloody Brother."

> **"People who fly into a rage seldom make a smooth landing."**
>
> —Anonymous
>
>
>
> **"Keep your head cool and your feet warm, and a glass of good whiskey will do you no harm."**
>
> Sir Walter Scott

A half-dozen gentlemen, feeling no pain, walked down the street at about one in the morning. Laughing and singing, they arrived at an attractive two-story home. One of them managed to get to the door and pound on it. A light came on in a second-story window. The leader of the pack bowed graciously and said, "Is this where Mr. Joseph smith lives?" "It is. What do you want?"

"Then, no doubt, I have the honor of speaking to Mrs. Smith. It that true?"

"I'm Mrs. Smith. What do you want?"

"Could you come down here and pick out Mr. Smith so the rest of us can go home?"

HAVE ANOTHER!

"**A mistake at least proves somebody stopped talking long enough to do something.**"

—Anonymous

"**If you want a place in the sun, you've got to expect a few blisters.**"

—Anonymous

The country doctor came in to see his patient in the hospital with a sad look on his face. "My friend," he said. "I've got some bad news and some worse news."

"Well, doc," said the patient, "hit me with the bad news first."

"You've only got but twenty-four hours to live."

"Doc," the patient gasped, "if that's the bad news, what's the worse news?"

The doctor hung his head and said "I was supposed to tell you yesterday."

—LORRAINE MORROW, FL

I walked in a bar the other day and ordered a double. The bartender brings out a guy who looks just like me.

"Excuse me," the party guest asked his hostess, "Do you have another lemon? I need to fix another drink."

"Another lemon? I don't have any lemons." "Are you sure?" "Of course I'm sure," the hostess said.

"Oh, my gawd," the guest groaned. "I think I squeezed your canary into my other drink."

~~~

While sleeping off a great night out, a fellow was a bit confused and called the sheriff and said, "Sheriff, someone took my steering wheel from my car."

The sheriff replied, "I will be over in about ten minutes." A few minutes later, the same fellow called the sheriff and said, "Sheriff, forget the report on the missing steering wheel, I was sitting in the back seat."

—CHARLES. R. BAXLEY, AR

A bartender is:

1. An irrigation engineer.
2. The only psychiatrist who works in an apron.
3. A good mixer in more ways than one.
4. A man who brings you in contact with the spirit world.
5. A man to whom almost everything is a stirring event.
6. One who knows that the emptiest men in the world are those that are full.

A Real HOOT!

My boss hired a new cocktail waitress, and I am sure it was only for her looks. She knew nothing about alcohol or mixed drinks, but, serving more than 400 dinners on Fridays and Saturdays, we needed all the help we could get. She came to the service window one particularly brutally busy Friday (her first night on the job) and asked me for a gin and tonic and a rum and coke. I poured both drinks for her and rushed back to the three-deep bar. She never took the drinks. I glanced over and asked her what was wrong. She said she didn't know which drink was which. Frustrated, I told her the lighter one was the gin and tonic. She picked up both drinks, held them at arms length, and insisted: "I still can't tell! They weigh the same!!"

> **"It's never too late to have a happy childhood."**
> —Anonymous
>
> **"A little folly now and then is cherished by the wisest of men."**
> —Anonymous

"MY EX-WIFE GOT THE LAST LAUGH!"

A **guy goes to the doctor** complaining of terrible aches and pains. The doctor gives him; a thorough work-up and sits the man down and says, "It doesn't look good. From what I can tell, you have an advanced case of herpes, a terrible rash, and syphilis. You also have German measles, poison oak, beriberi, pyorrhea, malaria, chicken pox, leprosy, not to mention sleeping sickness, typhus, diphtheria, and trench mouth."

"Doctor, what can I do?"

"We will place you in a special room in the hospital and feed you a special diet of pancakes and tortillas."

"And that will cure me?"

"No," says the doctor, "but it's the only food that we can slip under the door."

Three vampire bats fly into a bar. The first bat orders a blood.

"Ditto," says the second bat. The third bat asks the bartender for a plasma.

"Let me be sure I've got this right," says the bartender. "That will be a blood, a blood, and a blood lite."

> **"Bad men live that they may eat and drink, whereas good men eat and drink that they may live."**
>
> — Socrates

Joel and Craig are watching the latest launch of the space shuttle on the evening news in Smitty's Bar. "Do you think that there is intelligent life on other planets?" says Joel. "There has to be," says Craig.

"What makes you so sure?"

"Well, for one thing, you don't see them throwing away billions and billions of dollars looking for intelligent life down here!"

> ## "When the going gets tough, the tough get going."
>
> —Anonymous
>
>
>
> ## "If the headache would only precede the intoxication, alcoholism would be a virtue."
>
> — Samuel Butler

A man and giraffe walk into a bar and start drinking.

The giraffe passes out and the man gets up to leave.

The barman says, "You can't leave that lyin' there."

The man says, "It's not a lion, it's a giraffe."

ANOTHER ROUND!

> ## "Drink no longer water, but use a little wine for thy stomach's sake."
> — The New Testament
>
>
>
> ## "There is no such thing as a little garlic."
> —Anonymous

A doctor walks into a bar, sits down in front of the bartender and says, "Hey, aren't you sick and tired of people coming to you and telling you all their problems as if you were their therapist?" The bartender nodded in agreement. The next day the doctor was surprised to see the bartender in his office. When it was time to examine the bartender, the doctor called him in. The bartender walked into the examination room, sits down in front of the doctor and says, "Hey, aren't you sick and tired of people coming to you and..."

—Vivatcheil Chowchuvech, Clifton, NJ

"Major, I see two cocktails carried to your room every morning as if you had some one to drink with."

"Yes, sir, one cocktail makes me feel like another man; and of course, I'm bound to treat the other man."

The bartender presented the conventioneer with the bill, and the customer was outraged.

"New York is the most expensive place in the world," he complained. "Why, back in Sioux City, you can drink as much as you want without paying, sleep in a fancy hotel for free and wake up and find fifty dollars on your pillow."

"Come on, now," questioned the bartender. "Has that ever happened to you?"

"No," the man admitted, "but it happens to my wife all the time."

～～～

A man drowns in a vat at the brewery. When they told his wife, she asked, "Did he suffer?"

His companion replied, "No, he managed to get out and go to the men's room three times before he went under."

> ## "Drink today, and drown all sorrow;
> ## You shall perhaps not do it tomorrow."
> — John Fletcher

> ## "Bronze is the mirror of the form;
> ## wine, of the heart."
> — Aeschylus

An Easterner driving through Texas stopped late one night at a large motel with an adjoining tavern. Upon entering the latter, he noticed that the bar was extremely long and the bartender very tall. He asked for a short beer and was served a quart stein. When he commented on this, the bartender said, "Stranger, as you've probably heard, we do everything big here in Texas."

After a few beers the traveler asked where the john was. The bartender told him to take a corridor on the right to the last door on the left; but the man, a bit confused, walked down the corridor and through the last door on the right, which abutted on the motel swimming pool.

"My God!" He yelled as he thrashed wildly in the water. "Don't flush it! Don't flush it!"

> "Live in each season as it passes;
> breathe the air, drink the drink,
> taste the fruit and resign yourself
> to the influences of each."
>
> — Henry David Thoreau (1817-1862),
> American essayist, poet and naturalist

Counsel: (to police witness): "But if a man is on his hands and knees in the middle of the road that does not prove he has had too much to drink."

Cop: "No, sir, it does not, but this one was trying to roll up the white line."

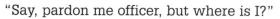

"Say, pardon me officer, but where is I?"

"You're on the corner of Broadway and Forty-Third, son."

"Cut out the details. Just what town am I in?"

> **"Doctors don't ask the right questions to find out whether you have a drink problem. They should ask things like 'Have you ever woken up on a plane to Turkey? Has Oliver Reed ever said to you, 'Push off mate, I'm going home now?' *That's* a drink problem."**
>
> — Jenny Lecoat

Two babies walk into a bar. One says to the other, "Ever get the feeling we're in the wrong joke?"

The clerk of a humble hotel said, "Would you like a room with running water?"

The man replied, "What do I look like? A trout?"

> ## "A heavy drinker is someone who drinks more than his doctor does."
>
> — Anonymous
>
>
>
> ## "This is a youth-oriented society, and the joke is on them because youth is a disease from which we all recover."
>
> —Anonymous

"Hey there," bellowed a policeman to a man, "You can't stand there in the street!"

"Yes, I can offisher," replied the man proudly. "Don't you worry about me, I been standing here an hour and ain't fell off yet."

CHEERS!

> **"Wouldn't it be terrible if I quoted some reliable statistics which prove that more people are driven insane through religious hysteria than by drinking alcohol?"**
>
> — W.C. Fields

> **"Before you borrow money from a friend, decide which you need more."**
>
> —Anonymous

> **"I know bourbon gets better with age, because the older I get, the more I like it."**
>
> — Booker Noe, Master Distiller and grandson of Jim Beam

A man walks into a bar and haltingly makes his way up to the counter. Clutching a stool he sits down and orders a double martini. When the drink arrives he grasps the glass with two hands and shakily raises the drink to his lips, spilling half the contents.

"Hey doc," says the man next to him, patting him on the shoulder. "What are you up to these days?"

"Same old thing," he says, wiping his lips, "brain surgery."

A pirate walked into a bar and the bartender said, "Hey, I haven't seen you in a while. What happened, you look terrible!"

"What do you mean? I'm fine."

"What about that wooden leg? You didn't have that before."

"Well," said the pirate, "We were in a battle at sea and a cannon ball hit my leg but the doc fixed me up and I'm fine."

"Oh yeah? What about that hook? The last time I saw you, you had both hands."

"We were in another battle and we boarded the enemy ship. I was in a swordfight and my hand was cut off, but Doc fixed me up with a hook and I feel great, really."

"Oh," said the bartender, "what about that eye patch? The last time you were in here you had both eyes."

"One day when we were at sea some birds were flying over the ship. I looked up and one of them crapped in my eye."

"You're kidding," said the bartender. "You couldn't have lost an eye just from some bird crap!"

"Well, I wasn't really used to the hook yet."

Two men met at a cocktail party, and as they stood talking, one glanced across the room and remarked, "Get a load of that ugly woman over there, with a nose like a pomegranate and what looks to be a fifty-five inch waistline."

"That's my wife," said the other man.

"Oh, I'm sorry," said the first man.

"*You're* sorry?"

A bartender placed a scotch and soda in front of a customer and announced, "That's the last one of those I'll serve today."

"What's the matter?" asked the customer, as he paid for his drink.

"Out of scotch?"

"No," explained the bartender, "but the place is on fire."

~~~

A man was hunched over in a suburban bar in Boston, tooth-pick in hand, spearing futilely at the olive in his drink. A dozen times the olive eluded him. Finally, the bartender, who had been watching intently, grabbed the toothpick. "Here, this is how you do it," he said, as he easily skewered the olive.

"Big deal, I had him so tired out he couldn't get away," barked the drunk.

> ## "If you're not confused, you're not paying attention."
> —Anonymous
>
> ———
>
> ## "Beer drinkin' don't do half the harm of love makin'."
> — Alexander Pope

> **"Always carry a flagon of whiskey in case of snakebite and furthermore always carry a small snake."**
>
> — W.C. Fields

A man with a penchant for alcoholic refreshment took a prescription from his doctor to his favorite bar. "What made you think I could fill this?" asked the bartender.

"Well," was the answer, "I want it in the gin–eric form."

> **"People who can agree on what's funny can usually agree on other things."**
>
> —Anonymous

> **"I never drink anything stronger than gin before breakfast."**
>
> — W.C. Fields

Young Miss Smith brought her mother into a local pub to meet her newest boyfriend, Joe the bartender. Mrs. Smith was unimpressed by the young man and began criticizing him right away.

As Joe poured the woman's drink, she shot him a very disapproving look. "I saw you use your hand to pick up that ice. I want a new drink."

"No, ma'am," Joe protested his innocence. "I would never use my hand for the ice."

Still, the old woman insisted she had seen what she had seen until Joe was forced to make her a new drink, conspicuously using tongs to handle the ice. But even that wasn't enough for the old woman, and she very loudly proclaimed to her daughter that, for all she knew, Joe could've returned from the men's room without washing his hands and she wasn't about to drink anything he had touched with his filthy hands.

More than a little annoyed, Joe told the old biddy she had nothing to worry about there, since he didn't need his hands to go to the men's room.

"Oh, really?" Mrs. Smith laughed derisively. "How's that?"

Joe let out a wicked smile. "That's what the tongs are for."

> ## "Enjoy today and don't waste it grieving over a bad yesterday—tomorrow may be even worse."
> —Anonymous
>
>
>
> ## "It's a long time between drinks."
> —Anonymous

"An Irishman driving down the road got pulled over by a policeman.

"You're drunk," the cop said.

"Thank the lord for that," the Irishman replied. "I thought the steering had gone."

~~~~~

GARY: "How'd you get them scars on your nose?"
HARRY: "From glasses!"
GARY: "Why not try contact lenses?"
HARRY: "They don't hold enough beer."

"NO, SORRY MA'AM.
THERE'S NOBODY HERE RIGHT NOW."

Thirsty?

IT'S 5:00 SOMEWHERE!

Have you ever wondered...

➤ If a parsley farmer is sued, can they 'garnish' his wages?

➤ If a stealth bomber crashes in a forest, will it make a sound?

➤ When it rains, why don't sheep shrink?

➤ If the cops arrest a mime, do they tell her she has the right to talk?

➤ Do you need a silencer if you're going to shoot a mime?

➤ Do cemetery workers prefer the graveyard shift?

➤ What do you do when you discover an endangered animal that eats only endangered plants?

➤ Is it possible to be totally partial?

➤ What's another word for thesaurus?

➤ When companies ship Styrofoam, what do they pack it in?

➤ Why are there flotation devices instead of parachutes under plane seats?

➤ Have you ever imagined a world with no hypothetical situations?

➤ How does the guy who drives the snowplow get to work in the morning?

➤ If 7-11 is open 24 hours a day, 365 days a year, why are there locks on the doors?

➤ If a cow laughed, would milk come out of its nose?

➤ If nothing ever sticks to Teflon, how do they make Teflon stick to the pan?

- If you're in a vehicle going the speed of light, what happens when you turn on the headlights?
- Why do they put Braille dots on the keypad of the drive-up ATM?
- Why do we drive on parkways and park on driveways?

Managing a new restaurant can be frustrating, even though business might be sensational. My restaurant hired a young man to help out on busy shifts. He was eager, at least. Serving one couple, I happened to hear some of his zealousness, by chance. After dinner, the husband ordered a Marie Brizzard cordial. The wife thought, and finally asked if we had any Irish coffee.

"No, ma'am," he replied. "All of our coffee comes from Colombia."

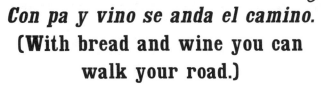

Con pa y vino se anda el camino.
(With bread and wine you can walk your road.)
—Spanish proverb

A waiter noticed that one of his customers kept buying quarts of beer and taking them into the men's room. Finally, he couldn't hold his curiosity any longer and followed the man to see what he was doing.

What the waiter saw really flipped him. The man was pouring the beer into the toilet.

"Say, what are you spilling good beer for?" he asked.

"Because I'm sick and tired of being just the middleman," was the answer.

> ## "Beer makes you feel the way you ought to feel without beer."
>
> — Henry Lawson
>
> ---
>
> ## "Who loves not wine, women, and song remains a fool his whole life long."
>
> —Anonymous

It's a little-known fact that William Tell and his son were avid bowlers as well as archery buffs. Unfortunately, all the league records were destroyed in a fire, so it may never be known for whom the Tells bowled.

HAVE ANOTHER!

> **"A cup of hot wine with not a drop of allaying Tiber in 't."**
> — William Shakespeare

> **"A joke that has to be explained is at its wit's end."**
> —Anonymous

A group of chess enthusiasts had checked into a hotel, and were standing in the lobby discussing their recent tournament victories. After about an hour, the manager came out of the office and asked them to disperse.

"But why?" they asked as they moved off. "Because," he said. "I can't stand chess nuts boasting in an open foyer."

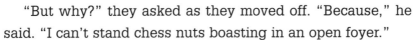

The old-timer, looking bent, weary and dejected, hobbled painfully up to the bar.

"What the trouble?" asked a kindly acquaintance. "You look bad."

"It's yoorz," moaned the old-timer. "I've got a bad case of yoorz."

"What's yoorz?" asked the puzzled friend.

"A double scotch, thanks."

Downright WACKY!

On the top of a tall building in a large city, there is a bar. In this bar, a man was drinking heavily. He would ask the bartender for a tequila shot, then walk out to the balcony and jump off. Minutes later, he would appear in the elevator and repeat the whole process. One guy watched this happen a number of times until curiosity got the better of him. Finally, he went up to the man and asked, "Hey, you keep drinkin', then jumpin' off the balcony. And yet, minutes later, you're back again. How do you do it?"

"Well, the shot of tequila provides a buoyancy such that when I get near the ground, I slow down and land gently! It's lots of fun. You should try it." The guy, who was also quite pissed out of his gourd, thought to himself, "Hey, why not?"

So he went to the bar, drank a shot of tequila, then walked out to the balcony, jumped off and whoooooo, splat! The bartender looked over at the first guy and said, "You are one mean drunk, Superman."

"The three-martini lunch is the epitome of American efficiency. Where else can you get an earful, a bellyful, and a snootful at the same time?"

— Gerald R. Ford

> **"I envy people who drink, at least they know what to blame everything on."**
>
> — Oscar Levant

> **"Do not allow children to mix drinks. It is unseemly and they use too much vermouth."**
>
> — Steve Allen

On the last day of school, the children brought gifts for the teacher. The florist's son brought the teacher a bouquet. The candy-store owner's daughter handed the teacher a pretty box of candy.

Then the liquor store owner's son brought up a big, heavy box. The teacher lifted it up and noticed that it was leaking a little bit. She touched a drop of liquid with her finger and tasted it.

"Is it wine?" She guessed.

"No," the boy replied.

She tasted another drop and asked, "Champagne?"

"No," said the little boy.

"I give up," she said. "What is it?"

"A puppy!"

A very important person came to the Smith's house one evening. Little Billy brought him a glass of sherry then stood staring at him.

"Please, will you do your trick for me now?" said he.

"What trick?" asked the V.I.P.

"Well, my dad says you can drink like a fish!"

> ### "What contemptible scoundrel has stolen the cork to my lunch?"
> — W.C. Fields
>
>
>
> ### "Good wine ruins the purse; bad wine ruins the stomach."
> — Spanish saying

EMPLOYER: "Mr. Jones, you disappoint me. I was told you were seen at the company party intoxicated and pushing a wheelbarrow."

JONES: "Why, yes, but I thought you approved."

EMPLOYER: "Of course not. Why would I approve?"

JONES: "Because you were riding in the wheelbarrow."

> **"Were I to prescribe a rule for drinking, it should be formed upon a saying quoted by Sir William Temple: 'the first glass for myself, the second for my friends, the third for good humor, and the fourth for mine enemies.'"**
>
> — Joseph Addison

A man walked into a bar with a pig under his arm. "Where on earth did you find that filthy animal?" asked the bartender.

"Oh, him? I bought him at an auction," replied the pig.

～～～

A thoroughly-married man managed to elude his wife and slip off to a neighborhood emporium, where he promptly asked for a pitcher of martinis.

"You mean a glass, don't you?" The bartender asked.

The customer looked enraged: "Now you're beginning to sound like my wife."

A judge was interviewing a woman regarding her pending divorce and asked, "What are the grounds for your divorce?"

She replied, "About four acres and a nice little home in the middle of the property with a stream running by."

"No," he said. "I mean, what is the foundation of this case?"

"It is made of concrete, brick and mortar," she responded.

"I mean," he continued, "what are your relations like?"

"I have an aunt and uncle living here in town, and so do my husband's parents."

He said, "Do you have a real grudge?"

"No," she replied. "We have a two-car carport and have never really needed one."

"Please," he tried again, "is there any infidelity in your marriage?"

"Yes, both my son and daughter have stereo sets. We don't necessarily like the music, but the answer to your question is yes."

"Ma'am, does your husband ever beat you up?"

"Yes," she responded. "About twice a week he gets up earlier than I do."

Finally in frustration the judge asked, "Lady, why do you want a divorce?"

"Oh, I don't want a divorce," she replied. "I've never wanted a divorce. My husband does. He said he can't communicate with me."

> "It takes seventeen muscles to smile and forty-three muscles to frown."
> —Anonymous

> "A tavern is a house kept for those who are not housekeepers."
> —Chatfield

A man was mounting a curb when he slipped and fell. A stranger was standing over him as he struggled to his feet.

"Did you see me fall?"

"Yes, I was standing right here. I saw you."

"Did you see me get up?"

"Yes, I saw you get up."

"Then what's my name?"

"How should I know your name? I never saw you before."

"Then how did you know that it was me that fell?"

A wino made a nuisance of himself, so the bartender picked him up and tossed him out into the street. A minute later, the wino was in again. Again, the bartender heaved him out. This happened a half-dozen times. Finally the wino said, "Do you work in every joint on this block?"

Joe was drinking his beer at the bar when his young son came in crying, "Daddy, Daddy, come home! Our house is burning down!"

When Joe calmly ordered another beer, the bartender asked, "Aren't you going to go home? Your house is on fire!"

"Oh, hell," Joe replied, "What's the big deal? I got enough lumber stored in my attic to build a whole new house!"

> **"Drink wine, and you will sleep well. Sleep, and you will not sin. Avoid sin, and you will be saved. Ergo, drink wine and be saved."**
>
> — Medieval German saying
>
>
>
> **"He was a wise man who invented beer."**
>
> — Plato

You sound like a duck...quack-quack-quack...

This duck walks into a bar and the bartender looks at him and says, "Hey, buddy, your pants are down..."

ANOTHER ROUND!

> ## "Life's only lasting joy comes in erasing the boundary line between 'mine' and 'yours.'"
> —Anonymous

Here's a ZINGER!

> ## "If you can't remember a joke— don't dismember it."
> —Anonymous

Bragging at the town bar, the farmer announced, "The man who marries my daughter will get a real prize."

"That sounds real interesting," said one of the youths. "What's the prize?"

~~~~~

A customs officer, while examining a sailor's baggage, discovered a bottle of whiskey. "I thought you told me there was only night clothes in that suitcase?"

"Right," replied the gob, "that's my night cap."

> ## "Life is too short to drink bad wine."
> — Winston Churchill

The case of the watered wine

The customer sat at the bar sipping his drink and watching as the bartender took two measured containers – holding a liter each – from under the sink. The bartender emptied the contents of the beakers down the drain, and refilled one with a liter of water and other with a liter of wine. He then transferred one cubic centimeter of the water to the beaker of wine and mixed them thoroughly. Then a cubic centimeter of the mixture was carefully transferred back to the beaker of water. Finally he turned to his customer and said: "I'll give you a drink on the house if you can tell me if there is now more water in the wine than wine in the water...or is there more wine in the water than water in the wine?" The customer won the free drink. What answer did he give the bartender? It works out this way...

The answer is that there is just as much wine in the water as water in the wine. The customer was able to answer because he knew that there was only one significant fact: at the end, each beaker held exactly as much liquid as it did at the beginning. Obviously, if "x" amount of wine was missing from the wine beaker, the space previously filled by the wine must now be filled with "x" amount of water. The reverse would be true in the case of the water beaker.

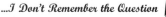

Two gentlemen of wealth settled down to an evening's drinking.

Having consumed the entire contents of one bottle, they decided to fetch up another. Checking through the host's supply – which included a number of dust-covered wine bins – they found a likely choice, a bottle of truly excellent whiskey.

"And how old do you think this is?" the guest asked.

"Doesn't say on the label," the host replied, "but it's as old as it's ever going to be."

> **"He is not an honest man who has burned his tongue and does not tell the company that the soup is hot."**
>
> —Anonymous
>
>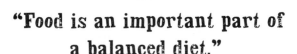
>
> **"Food is an important part of a balanced diet."**
>
> — Fran Lebowitz

A duck walks into a bar and says, "I'll take a shot of bourbon, and put it on my bill…"

CHEERS!

Guy walks into a bar, puts his briefcase on the bar, orders a shot. Asks the bartender if he can have a tiny shot poured into a bottle cap for his little buddy, and he opens his briefcase to show a foot-high man, alive, sitting at a piano playing tunes. The bartender is amazed and asks "Where did you find this guy?"

The customer points to a magic lantern also in his briefcase and said, "I made a wish to the genie in this lantern."

The bartender is thrilled and asks if he can make a wish. The guy says sure, so the bartender rubs the lantern. A genie emerges and asks, "What is your wish?"

The bartender says, "I wish I had a million bucks."

In a flash, the bar is packed floor to ceiling with thousands of squawking ducks.

The bartender screams "Ducks! I said bucks! Bucks! Is this genie deaf or something?"

The customer screams, "You didn't think I asked for a twelve-inch pianist, did you?"

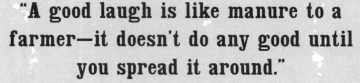

"A good laugh is like manure to a farmer—it doesn't do any good until you spread it around."

—Anonymous

A lady walks into a bar with a duck under her arm. A drunk at the bar looks up and says "Where did you get that pig?"

The lady barks back at the drunk saying "That's not a pig, that's a duck!"

The drunk says "I wasn't talking to you, I was talking to the duck."

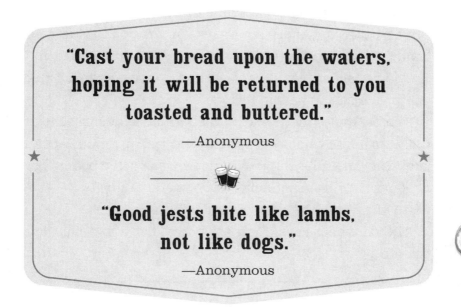

"Cast your bread upon the waters, hoping it will be returned to you toasted and buttered."

—Anonymous

"Good jests bite like lambs, not like dogs."

—Anonymous

This guy walks into a bar with a duck on his head. The bartender, who's seen just about everything says, "What can I get you?"

To which the duck replies, "You can start by getting this guy off my ass."

A **bear walks into a bar** in Billings, Montana and sits down. He bangs on the bar with his paw and demands a beer. The bartender approaches him and says, "We don't serve beer to bears in bars in Billings."

The bear, becoming angry, demands again that he be served a beer. The bartender tells him again, more forcefully, "We don't serve beer to belligerent bears in bars in Billings."

The bear, very angry now, says, "If you don't serve me a beer, I'm going to eat that lady sitting at the end of the bar."

The bartender says, "Sorry, we don't serve beer to belligerent, bully bears in bars in Billings."

The bear goes to the end of the bar, and as promised, eats the woman. He comes back to his seat and again demands a beer. The bartender states, "Sorry, we don't serve beer to belligerent, bully bears in Billings who are on drugs."

The bear says, "I'm not on drugs!"

The bartender says, "You are now. That was a bar bitch you ate."

> **"Woman is the lesser man, and all thy passions, match'd with mine, are as moonlight unto sunlight, and as water unto wine."**
>
> — Alfred Lord Tennyson

The man lay prostrate in the middle of the road early Sunday morning when two men came straggling by. "He's drunk out of his mind," said one.

"He ain't drunk at all," mumbled the other drunk. "I just seen his fingers move."

> ## "Up to the age of forty eating is beneficial. After forty, drinking."
> — The Talmud (200 B.C.)
>
>
>
> ## "Wine is the most helpful and most hygienic of beverages."
> — Louis Pasteur

McGee and his friend staggered out of Malloy's, appropriated a brand-spanking-new Cadillac, and went tearing up Broadway at the height of the theatre crush at sixty miles an hour.

"This is terrible," cried the passenger. "I can't stand it!"

"Okay then," counseled McGee. "Just close your eyes, like I'm doing."

> ## "If life is a waste of time, and time is a waste of life, then let's all get wasted together and have the time of our lives."
>
> – Armand's Pizza, Washington, DC

> ## "Remember, it's not, 'How high are you?' It's 'Hi, how are you?'"
>
> – Rest stop off Route 81, WV

A prim little lady was telling her friend about the awful shock of finding two empty whiskey bottles in her garbage can.

"You can imagine my embarrassment," she said, "I got them out fast because I didn't want the garbage man to think I drink."

"What did you do with them?" asked the friend.

"Well, the minister lives next door," was the reply. "So I put them in his garbage can. Everybody knows he doesn't drink."

> ## "Abstinence is a good thing, but it should always be practiced in moderation."
>
> —Anonymous

A redhead, a brunette, and a blonde walk into a bar. The bartender asks the redhead what she would like. She says, "I'll have a a.l." The bartender looks lost, and so the redhead says, "Duuuuhh, an Amstel Lite!"

Next, the bartender asks the brunette what she would like. The brunette says, "I'll have a b.l." With this, the bartender gets a grin on his face and says, "Bud Lite, right?"

The brunette says, "Duuuuhh, Beck's Lite! " Feeling really dumb, he asks the blonde what she would like to drink. The blonde says, "I'll have a 15."

The bartender says to himself, "A 15, a 15, a 15?"

The blonde says, "Duuuuhh, a 7 and 7!"

> **"Evidence...proves that prohibition only drives drunkenness behind doors and into dark places, and does not cure it or even diminish it."**
>
> — Mark Twain

"Why do you beg?"

"The truth is, I beg to get money to drink."

"Why do you drink?"

"To give me the courage to beg."

HAVE ANOTHER!

McGee was finally cornered by his wife in a bar where he was dreamily contemplating a slug of whiskey. Being in a genial mood, he offered her a sip, but when she took it she gagged and sputtered, finally coming out with, "How can you ever drink that horrible stuff?"

"See, I told you," said McGee. "And all the while you thought I was having a good time!"

> **"When men drink, then they are rich and successful and in lawsuits and are happy to help their friends. Quickly, bring me a beaker of wine, so that I may wet my mind and say something clever."**
>
> — Aristophanes c. 450-385 B. Knights (424 B.C.) l. 92

Three deaf ladies were traveling on top of an open bus. "Windy, isn't it?" said one.

"No, it isn't Wednesday, it's Thursday," said the second.

"Yes, I'm thirsty too. Let's all get off and have something to drink," said the third.

It's a taffy-pulling contest at St. Peter's, not a peter-pulling contest at St. Taffy's. (Signs you have had too many.)

➤ You lose arguments with inanimate objects.

➤ You have to hold onto the lawn to keep from falling off the earth.

➤ Your job is interfering with your drinking.

➤ Your doctor finds traces of blood in your alcohol stream.

➤ Your career won't progress beyond senator from Massachusetts.

➤ The back of your head keeps getting hit by the toilet seat.

➤ You sincerely believe alcohol to be the elusive 5th food group.

➤ 24 hours in a day, 24 beers in a case, coincidence? I think not!

➤ Two hands and just one mouth – now that's a problem!

➤ You can focus better with one eye closed.

➤ The parking lot seems to have moved while you were in the bar.

➤ Every woman you see has an exact twin.

➤ You fall off the floor…

➤ Your twin sons are named Barley and Hops.

➤ Hey, 5 beers has just as many calories as a burger, screw dinner!

- The glass keeps missing your mouth!
- Vampires and mosquitoes catch a buzz after attacking you.
- Your idea of cutting back is less salt.
- The whole bar says "hi" when you come in.
- You think the four basic food groups are caffeine, nicotine, alcohol and women/men.
- Every night you're beginning to find your roommate's cat more and more attractive.
- Hi ocifer. I'm not under the affluence of incohol.
- You don't recognize your wife unless seen through bottom of glass.
- That damned pink elephant followed me home again.
- Senators Kennedy and Packwood shake their heads when they walk past you.
- You have a reserved parking space at the liquor store.
- You wake up in Korea in August and the last thing you remember is the Fourth of July party at the Halekulani in Waikiki.
- You've fallen and you can't get up.

> **"The best way for a person to have happy thoughts is to count his blessings and not his cash."**
>
> —Anonymous

Knee Slapper!

Mitch and Mary had only been married for two weeks. Mitch, although very much in love, couldn't wait to go out into town and party with his old buddies. So he says to his new wife, "Honey, I'll be right back…"

"Where are you going, coochy cooh…?" asked Mary.

"I'm going to the bar, pretty face. I'm going to have a beer."

Mary says to him, "You want a beer, my love?" Then she opens the door to the refrigerator and shows him twenty-five different kinds of beer brands from twelve different countries: Germany, Holland, Japan, India, and so on.

Mitch doesn't know what to do, and the only thing he can think of saying is, "Yes, loolie…but the bar…you know…the frozen glass…"

He didn't get to finish the sentence, when Mary interrupts him by saying, "You want a frozen glass, puppy face?" She takes a huge beer mug out of the freezer so frozen that she was getting chills holding it.

Mitch, looking a bit pale, says, "Yes, tootsie roll, but at the bar they have those hors d'oeuvres that are really delicious...I won't be long. I'll be right back. I promise. Okay?"

"You want hors d'oeuvres poochy-pooh?" She opens the oven and takes out fifteen dishes of different hors d'oeuvres: chicken wings, pigs in a blanket, mushroom caps, pork strips, and the like.

"But sweet honey...at the bar...you know...the swearing, the dirty words and all that..."

"You want dirty words, cutie pie? Here—drink your damn beer in your damn frozen glass and eat your damn hors d'oeuvres, cause you aren't going anywhere, asshole!"

> **"Moderation is a fatal thing— nothing succeeds like excess."**
> — Oscar Wilde
>
>
>
> **"Not what we have, but what we enjoy, constitutes our abundance."**
> —Anonymous

The immigrant had promised his friends in the old country that he was going to have a drink in the best bar in America when he got to New York. When he arrived he asked a policeman where the best bar was and he was directed to one.

He was awed when he got inside. Truly it was a sumptuous place, glittering chandeliers, ankle deep plush rugs, a sea of mirrors giving a jewel-like sparkle to the place. Strangely, the long bar was unoccupied. Two bartenders stood at the far end of the bar. The man waited patiently but the two bartenders didn't budge. Finally, the man's patience reached the breaking point.

"Do you serve beer here?" he shouted to the bartender.

"No, we serve jackasses here," the one bartender called.

"You must be doing pretty good with that," the immigrant said. "seeing as there are only you two left!"

> "Laugh and the world laughs with you. Cry and you get all wet."
>
> —Anonymous

> "True happiness may be sought, thought, or caught—but never bought."
>
> —Anonymous

ANOTHER ROUND!

A cowboy rode into town and stopped at the saloon for a drink. Unfortunately, the locals had a habit of always picking on newcomers. When the cowboy finished his drink, he found his horse had been stolen.

He went back into the bar, handily flipped his gun into the air, caught it above his head without even looking and fired a shot into the ceiling.

"Who stole my horse?" he yelled with surprising forcefulness.

No one answered.

"I'm gonna have another beer and if my horse ain't back outside by the time I'm finished, I'm gonna do what I dun back in Texas and I don't want to have to do what I dun back in Texas!" Some of the locals shifted restlessly. He had another beer, walked outside, and his horse was back! He saddled up and started to ride out of town.

The bartender wandered out of the bar and asked "Say, partner, what happened in Texas?"

The cowboy turned back and said, "I had to walk home."

"Burgundy for kings, champagne for duchesses, claret for gentlemen."

— Anonymous French Proverb

"**Happiness consists of living each day as if it were the first day of your honeymoon and the last day of your vacation.**"

—Anonymous

Here's a ZINGER!

"**A woman's rule of thumb: if it has tires or testicles, you're going to have trouble with it.**"

– Woman's restroom, Dick's Last Resort, Dallas, TX

"**The telephone is a good way to talk to people without having to offer them a drink.**"

— Fran Lebowitz

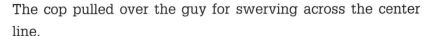

The cop pulled over the guy for swerving across the center line.

"You drinking?" asked the cop.

"Depends," the man replied. "You buyin'?"

Bad day

A **man was sitting at a bar,** just looking at his drink. After he didn't move for a half an hour, this big truck driver stepped up right next to him, took the drink from the guy, and just drank it.

The man started crying. The truck driver turned and said, "Come on pal, I was just joking. Here, I'll buy you another drink. I just can't stand to see a grown man crying."

"No, it's not that. Today is the worst day of my life. First, I overslept and was late for work. My boss became outraged and then fired me. When I left the building to my car, I found out that it was stolen. The police said they could do nothing. I then got a cab to return home, and after I paid the cab driver and the cab had gone, I found that I left my wallet in the cab. I got home only to find my wife in bed with the mailman. I left home depressed and came to this bar. And now, when I was thinking about putting an end to my life, you show up and drink my poison…"

> ## "Faith, hope, and charity—if you had more of the first two we'd need less of the last."
>
> —Anonymous

> **"Wine makes a man better pleased with himself; I do not say that it makes him more pleasing to others."**
>
> — Samuel Johnson

This snail crawls up to a bar that was closing. The snail pounds and pounds on the door until the bartender finally opens the door. The bartender looks around and notices nothing, until the snail demands a beer. The bartender looks down and sees him, but replies, "Hey, we're closed now and besides, we don't serve snails!" He then proceeds to slam the door.

The snail again pounds on the door until the bartender gets so frustrated that he opened the door again and kicks the snail away.

A year passes, and the bartender is closing again when he hears a pounding on the door again. He opens the door, looks down, and sees the same snail again!

The snail looks up and replies, "Why'd you have to go and do *that*?"

"I'm supposed to be repairing the lawn mower," a patron said to the bartender.

"Then what are you doing here?"

"I told my wife I needed a screwdriver."

> **"When I have one martini, I feel bigger, wiser, taller. When I have the second, I feel superlative. When I have more, there's no holding me."**
>
> — William Faulkner

> **"Enjoy yourself. These are the 'good old days' you're going to miss in the years ahead."**
>
> —Anonymous

A man walks into a bar carrying a door. "Why are you carrying that door?" asked the bartender.

"Well, last night, I lost my keys, so I'm carrying around the door in case somebody finds them and tries to break into my house."

CHEERS!

> ### "Our constitution protects aliens, drunks and U.S. senators."
> — Will Rogers
>
>
>
> ### "One good turn gets most of the blanket."
> —Anonymous

"Sometimes," said Mrs. McGee to the new maid, "it will be necessary for you to help me upstairs."

"I understand, ma'am," replied the girl. "I drink a bit myself."

"No matter how good she looks, some other guy is sick and tired of putting up with her crap."

– Men's room, Linda's Bar and Grill, Chapel Hill, NC

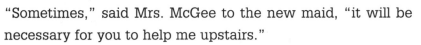

> "Laughter is like changing a baby's diaper—it doesn't permanently solve any problems, but it makes things more acceptable for a while."
>
> —Anonymous

A Real Scream!

It was a usual, busy weekend night. Everybody busy, music blaring, everybody going crazy. The old lady was back again. She'd been driving Harry the bartender bonkers for nights talking on and on about reincarnation; who she'd been in a previous life, and who she wanted to be the next time around.

"Harry!" she called. "Harry, over here!"

Harry hurried down the bar. "Another martini?"

"No; I just wanted to finish our conversation about reincarnation."

Harry started to move off. He said, "I'm busy, I can't stop now."

"Wait a minute," she cried. "I just want to ask you. Who do you want to be when you come back?"

Harry thought for a moment, threw up his hands, and yelled above the racket, "if I have anything to say about it, I'm gonna come back as a customer!"

When I was a little boy, I had but a little wit,
'Tis a long time ago, and I have no more yet;
Nor ever ever shall, until that I die,
For the longer I live the more fool am I.

—A<small>NONYMOUS</small>

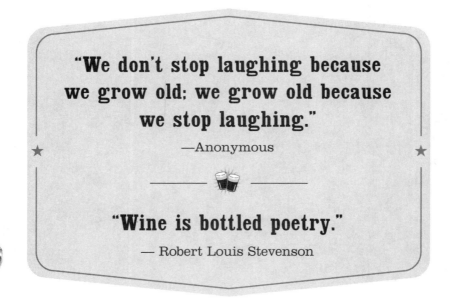

"We don't stop laughing because we grow old; we grow old because we stop laughing."

—Anonymous

"Wine is bottled poetry."

— Robert Louis Stevenson

The local drunk in a small town staggered out of a bar, gazing around in a befuddled manner. He spotted the town's only taxicab in front of the bar and climbed in. "Take me to Malloy's Place, driver," he said.

"Buddy, you're in front of Malloy's Place now," replied the driver.

"Okay, Mac," said the drunk as he staggered out of the cab. "But the next time, don't drive so blamed fast!"

Rover

A guy walks into a bar with his dog and says, "I'll have a scotch and water and my dog would like a beer."

The bartender says, "Sorry, we don't serve animals in here." The dog replies, "Hey, I'm tired of being discriminated against. Just give me a drink."

The bartender says, "Oh, no, not another ventriloquist with the old talking dog trick. Both of you, get out of here!"

"No, no, no, this isn't a trick, I promise you," says the man. "I tell you what, I'll go for a walk around the block and you talk to pal here."

The man leaves and the bartender sees him turn the corner. "Now, can I have my drink?" says the dog.

The bartender is amazed. "Sure you can and it's on the house! Listen, can you do me a favor? My wife works next door at the café. It'll make her day if you go in and order a cup of coffee. Here's five bucks and you can keep the change afterwards."

"Okay," says the dog and he takes the money and leaves.

Minutes go by and the dog doesn't come back. The owner returns and asks where the dog is. So both of them go off to see what happened to the dog. As they approach the café, they see Pal going at it hot and heavy with a French poodle in the alley between the bar and café. The owner shouts, "Pal, what are you doing? You've never done this before!"

The dog shrugs, "I've never had any money before."

> ## "In a restaurant choose a table near a waiter."
> — Jewish Proverb
>
>
>
> ## "Whoever tells the truth is chased out of nine villages."
> —Anonymous

A very shy bear goes into a bar and sees a beautiful woman sitting at the bar. After an hour of gathering up his courage, he finally goes over to her and asks tentatively, "Um, would you mind if I chatted with you for a while?"

To which she responds by yelling, at the top of her lungs, "No, I won't sleep with you tonight!"

Everyone in the bar is now staring at them. Naturally, the guy is hopelessly and completely embarrassed and he slinks back to his table. After a few minutes, the woman walks over to him and apologizes. She smiles at him and says, "I'm sorry if I embarrassed you. You see, I'm a graduate student in psychology and I'm studying how people respond to embarrassing situations."

To which he responds, at the top of his lungs, "What do you mean, $200?"

Have you heard about the new drink called card table?
Drink two of them and your legs fold up under you.

On average, how much cash do sports fans spend on beer?
A staggering amount.

> **"We are living in a world where lemonade is made from artificial flavors and furniture polish is made from real lemons."**
> — Alfred E. Newman

> **"Children are a great help. They are a comfort in your old age. And they help you reach it faster, too."**
> —Anonymous

Ice Cold Beer

The temperance lecturer had rented a hall for the evening, and he was discoursing on evils of rum.

"Now supposing I had a pail of water and a pail of rum on this platform, and then brought in a donkey; which one of them would he take?"

"He'd take the water," came the cry from McGee in the back.

"And why would he take the water?" asked the preacher.

"Because he's an ass," came the reply.

> ## "Worry doesn't help tomorrow's troubles, but it does ruin today's happiness."
>
> —Anonymous
>
>
>
> ## "The best way to a man's heart is to saw his breastplate open."
>
> – Women's restroom, Murphy's, Champaign, Il

"Excuse me, bartender, do you serve women here?"

"No, chum, you'll have to bring your own!"

HAVE ANOTHER!

This guy walks into a bar, sits down, and asks the bartender for a beer. The bartender gives the guy a beer. The guy drinks it, then reaches into his pocket, pulls something out, looks at it, puts it back, then asks the bartender for a scotch on the rocks.

The bartender gives it to him. The guy drinks it and reaches into his pocket. The bartender again notices him pull something out, look at it, and put it back. The guy looks over at the bartender and asks for a beer *and* a scotch on the rocks The bartender gives him the drinks.

The guy drinks them, reaches in his pocket, pulls something out, looks at it, and before he can put it back the bartender asks him, "Hey man, I'm curious here. I wanna know what you keep pulling out of your pocket."

The guy says to the bartender, "It's a picture of my wife. I keep checking it and when it starts looking good, I'm going home."

> **"Real friends are those who upon watching you make a fool of yourself do not feel that the job was done permanently."**
>
> —Anonymous

Two men were walking their dogs. One had a Doberman; the other had a Pekingese. They passed a bar and thought about going in, but figured that the bartender wouldn't let them in with the dogs, and if they left the dogs outside, they would be stolen.

The man with the Doberman said, "Follow me."

He went into the bar, and when the bartender stopped him he said, "Seeing-eye dog."

The bartender said, "Ok, come on in."

The man with the Pekingese went in, and the bartender stopped him, saying "No dogs."

The man said, "Seeing-eye dog."

The bartender said, "A *Pekingese*?"

The man said, "What the hell! Did they give me a Pekingese??"

"Customers who consider our waitresses uncivil ought to see the manager."

—Sign in a New York restaurant

"Open 7 days a week and weekends."

—Sign in a Maine restaurant

An elderly **woman goes to the doctor** and asks his help to revive her husband's sex drive. "What about trying Viagra?" asks the doctor.

"Not a chance," says Mrs. Murphy. "He won't even take an aspirin for a headache."

"No problem," replies the doctor. "Drop it in his cocktail, he won't even taste it. Try it and come back in a week to let me know how it goes."

A week later Mrs. Murphy returns to the doctor and he inquires as to how things went. "Oh, it was terrible, just horrible, doctor."

"What happened?" asks the doctor.

"Well, I did as you advised and slipped it in his cocktail. The effect was immediate. He jumped straight up, swept everything off the table in one big swoop while at the same time ripping my clothes off, and then proceeded to make passionate love to me on the tabletop. It was terrible."

"What was terrible and horrible?" said the doctor. "Was the sex not good?"

"Oh, no doctor, the sex was the best I've had in twenty-five years. But I'll never be able to show my face in that bar again."

A bull came into a bar and ordered a drink. When the bartender handed him the bill, he charged it.

A thirsty **gentleman** wandered into a corner saloon and ordered a dry martini. He drank it with evident relish, and allowed as how it was the best darn martini he had ever tasted in his life.

"Do you always mix them this way," he asked, "or was this one of those divine accidents?"

The barkeep whipped up another one as proof, and the customer declared it was even better than the first.

"Such genius deserves a reward," said the customer. He reached into his pocket and produced a live lobster, which he pressed into the hands of the astonished barkeep. "Here, take this. With my compliments!" he said.

The barkeep held the live crustacean gingerly at arm's length. "Thanks," he said dubiously. "I suppose I can take it home for dinner?"

"No, no," objected the customer. "He's already had his dinner. Take him to a movie."

"God made only water, but man made wine."

— Victor Hugo

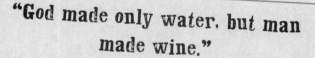

"Even if there is nothing to laugh about, laugh on credit."

—Anonymous

> **"Hope sees the invisible, feels the intangible and achieves the impossible. "If it were not for hope, the heart would break."**
>
> —Anonymous

Here's a ZINGER!

> **"A friend is one who warns you."**
>
> —Anonymous

A man is sitting at the bar when a priest comes in and taps him on the shoulder. "Excuse me, brother, do you love your neighbor?" He asks.

"Oh, I tried to," said the man, "but she won't let me."

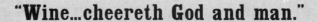

In Vino Veritas, in Cervesio Felicitas.
(In wine there is wisdom, in beer there is joy.)

> **"Wine...cheereth God and man."**
>
> — Judges 9:13

McGee had been advised by his doctor that if he did not give up whiskey it would shorten his life.

"Think so?" asked McGee.

"I am sure of it, McGee. If you stop drinking, I am sure it will prolong your life."

"Come to think of it, I believe you are right about that, doctor," replied McGee. "I went twenty-four days without a drink a year ago, and I never put in such a long day in my life."

"Beauty is only a light switch away."

–Perkins Library, Duke University, Durham, NC

"You're too good for him."

– Sign over a mirror in the women's room,
Ed Debevic's, Beverly Hills, CA

Mrs. McGee left her gloves, as usual, in the restaurant. She discovered her loss at the door and turned back. They weren't on the table, so she got down on all fours and began to search underneath.

A waiter tapped her on the shoulder. "If it's your husband you're looking for, madam," he said respectfully, "I think you'll find him in the washroom."

CHEERS!

> **"There are many good reasons for drinking,**
> **And one has just entered my head,**
> **If a man cannot drink when he's living**
> **How the hell can he drink when he's dead?"**
>
> —Anonymous

A man well known to the police was brought up before a magistrate who knew him well.

"McGee," said the judge, "You are charged with habitual drunkenness. What have you to offer in your defense?"

"Habitual thirst, your honor."

"But how on earth did you come to get so completely intoxicated?"

"Well, you see, it's like this, your honor. I got into bad company. There were four of us. I had a bottle of whiskey and the other three don't touch the stuff."

~~~

JUDGE: "McGee, you are here for intoxication."

MCGEE: "Fine, bring on the hooch!"

The man reeled out of the bar and stumbled into a taxi that was waiting at the curb. "I wanna go around this park thirty-one times," he informed the cabby. The driver noted that the man was extremely well dressed. He figured that his was not to reason why. He started driving around the park at a leisurely pace.

After about a mile he was stopped by a red light. His fare banged on the window and demanded angrily, "Faster, you damn fool. Can't you see I'm in a terrible hurry?"

"Friends don't let friends take home ugly men."

– Women's restroom, Starboard, Dewey Beach, DE

"No wonder you always go home alone."

– Sign over a mirror in the men's room, Ed Debevic's, Beverly Hills, CA

"How much better is thy love than wine!"

— Song of Solomon, 4:10

> ## "A man of courage never needs weapons, but he may need bail."
> —Anonymous
>
>
>
> ## "The world always looks brighter from behind a smile."
> —Anonymous

An IRS agent was bawling out a bartender, "You should have kept a record of every penny you made in tips."

"I don't know why you're getting so excited," says the bartender, "I hardly ever get pennies."

~~~~

Father Callahan was at a pitch of fervor in his sermon on drinking. "What could be worse than drink?" he boomed "Thirst!" shouted Brower from the rear.

"WHAT ARE YOU LAUGHING AT?"

Two hydrogen atoms walk into a bar. One says "I think I've lost an electron."

The other says "Are you sure?"

The first says, "Yeah, I'm positive."

～～～

Why was booze invented?

Because ugly people want love too.

～～～

Q: Did you hear about the new restaurant on the moon?

A: Great food but no atmosphere.

> ## "Conscience: something that feels terrible when everything else feels swell."
>
> —Anonymous

"Waiter - hiccup - bring me a - hiccup - dish of prunes."

"Stewed, sir?"

"That's none of your business!"

> **"There is a tavern in the town
> And there my true love sits
> him down
> And drinks his wine with
> laughter and glee
> And never, never thinks of me."**
>
> — Anonymous

"Lipchitz does other things beside drink."

"What's that?"

"He hiccups!"

~~~~~

I'd rather get a shot from my bartender than my doctor any day.

"Hell is truth seen too late."

—Anonymous

"With wine comes truth."

—Anonymous

Your Bar Jokes Go Here!

Your Bar Jokes Go Here!

....

....

....

....

....

....

....

....

About the Author

Ray Foley has been a bartender for more years than he wants to admit. He is the publisher of *Bartender* Magazine and the author of *Bartending for Dummies*, *How to Run a Bar for Dummies*, *The Best Irish Drinks*, *The Ultimate Little Martini Book*, and *The Ultimate Little Shooter Book*. He has appeared on numerous television shows and has had articles published in many national magazines. Ray resides in New Jersey with his wife and partner, Jaclyn, and his son Ryan. He can be contacted on his website, www.bartender.com or his e-mail, Barmag@aol.com.